DATE			

A BLAZING FOUNTAIN

A BLAZING FOUNTAIN

A BOOK FOR HANUKKAH

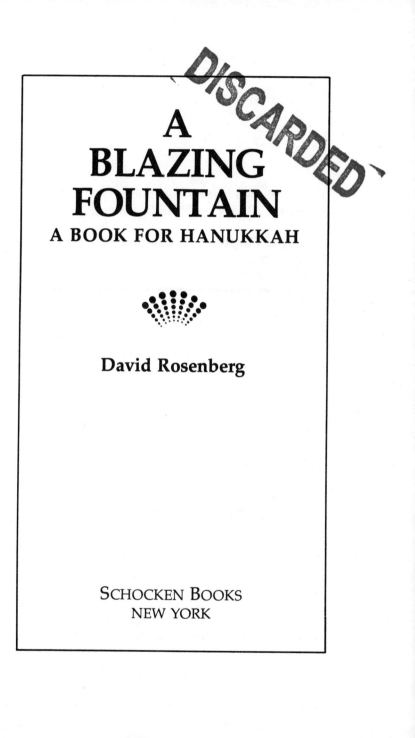

David Rosenberg

SCHOCKEN BOOKS
NEW YORK

First published by Schocken Books 1978
Copyright © 1978 by David Rosenberg

Library of Congress Cataloging in Publication Data
Main entry under title:
A Blazing fountain.
     1. Hanukkah (Feast of Lights)—History—
Sources.   I. Rosenberg, David.
BM695.H3B55   296.4'35   78–54388

Manufactured in the United States of America

Acknowledgments
Portions of these works first appeared in *Shefa Quarterly* (Jerusalem) and *Ah'shav* (Tel Aviv). "A Blazing Fountain (A Hanukkah Haftorah)" was first printed *hors commerce* as a broadside by Myra Klahr. Psalms 30 and 121 appeared in *Blues of the Sky* (New York: Harper & Row, 1976), © by David Rosenberg. Reprinted by permission.

Without the special encouragement of the following persons, this book would not have been composed: Shifra Rosenberg Asarch, David Rose, Myra Klahr, Moshe Greenberg, Nessa Rapoport, Naamah Kelman, Moshe Shur, Mimi Gross Grooms, Leslie Miller, Heide Lange, Barbara Rogan, Dominique and Miro Cole, and Seymour Barofsky.

In memory of
Benjamin Glazer
and Herman Rosenberg

CONTENTS

INTRODUCTION: The Maccabean
Imagination   1
THE BOOK OF JUDITH: A Modern
Version   15
from FIRST BOOK OF MACCABEES   47
from SECOND BOOK OF MACCABEES   67
from THE BOOK OF DANIEL   77
A BLAZING FOUNTAIN   89

Zechariah
from the Torah
Kings
Ezra
from the Hallel

ILLUMINATIONS   113

Lighting the Menorah
The Little Prayer for First Night
   Only (Shehecheyanu)
These Singing Lights
   (Hanerot Hallalu)
Rock of All My Dreams
   (Maoz Tzur)
We Remember the Miraculous
   (Al Hanissim)

vii

from the Talmud (Shabbat 21b)
Psalm for Making Hanukkah
   (Psalm 30)
Psalm from a "Great Hallel"
   (Psalm 121)

from ECCLESIASTES   145

An Old/New Vision of
   Hanukkah

A Note on Translation and Liturgy   175

INTRODUCTION

The Maccabean Imagination

THE MACCABEAN IMAGINATION

Today, as in Maccabean times, Hanukkah is probably the most sophisticated Jewish festival. The ideas associated with it confront the history of Western civilization. The spirit associated with it confronts the basis of universal religions and ideologies. And this is the Jewish holiday that is least understood by Americans, many of whom think of it as a nostalgic children's holiday, a quaint, Jewish reflection in the mirror of Christmas time.

Or perhaps it is thought of as commemorating an ancient military victory. But Hanukkah does not fit simplistic stereotypes. Early Christianity preserved another stereotype, recognizing Jewish martyrs of the Maccabean era as types of saints and the Maccabees themselves as righteous crusaders. Unfortunately these images had little effect on the popular, less noble distortions of the Jew.

Many stories and legends of Hanukkah have served different times and places. A recent one comes from comparing the Maccabean revolt to the Jewish revolt against the British in Palestine. But this analogy cannot convey all of the spiritual and cultural dimensions that sustained

Hanukkah through twenty-two centuries. Since the first Hanukkah, in 164 B.C.E., the festival has been clothed in nuance: the surest way to reveal its richness is to return to original sources.

The book *A Blazing Fountain* doesn't refer to every single source, but the ones I felt indispensable. The first four sections were composed near the Maccabean era (second century B.C.E.)—the Book of Judith and the Book of Daniel before the Maccabean revolt, and the two Books of Maccabees after Judean independence. The section itself entitled "A Blazing Fountain" sharpens the focus on Hanukkah: its roots in a deeper dimension of history than the Maccabean era, illuminating Jewish identity in the Torah, Prophets, and sacred literature.

During the eight days of Hanukkah, "Illuminations" is the key to the festival—containing the home celebration—and should be read first. This section is a handbook to the profoundly simple service of lighting a menorah, with its deep echoes in Jewish memory. The other sections, which give shape to the spirit of Hanukkah, can be read before or after the lights are burning.

The concluding section, from Ecclesiastes, reflects the most sublime dimension of the Maccabean imagination. While the observance of Hanukkah is partly a domestication of the ancient Temple rituals of Sukkot, it remains a vehicle for confronting the naked awe of God that brought Israel to Jerusalem. Just as the renewed Israel of our time, containing both religious and secular Jews, transcends those categories in its universal relevance to the Jewish Diaspora, Hanukkah also contains its seemingly opposite poles, bursting the bounds of observance in either a religious or secular context. Today, Ecclesiastes is the book of the Bible that perhaps most accurately reflects this down-to-earth synthesis of spirit.

We begin with the Book of Judith. When you lay this book beside the journalese of "retold" Hanukkah stories and bloodless American celebrations, it is striking to see how passionate an authentic Hanukkah text can be. Judith embodies the Maccabean imagination in its heady combination of irony and directness. Yet, fifty years ago, an imposing intelligence like Alfred North Whitehead could characterize the entire Hebrew Bible and Apocrypha as devoid of an ounce of humor. And that kind of ignorance, out of a sense of detached superiority, is no less widespread today. It comes from reading without a feeling for context and tradition—satire is difficult to grasp when you don't know whom or what is being played upon. For instance, the sober tone of Ecclesiastes is often mistaken for its essence. And irony is lost on an ear closed to the play on words and forms that is so rich in

ancient Hebrew literature. Judith is typical for
its delight in language and irony, even as its
tone is relentlessly serious. For example, the
Lord is invoked as a "crusher of wars," and then
Judith herself—in all ways the opposite of a
warrior hero—becomes instrumental in doing
just that. As the enemy flees the battlefield, the
Jews who give chase are mere "mamas' boys."

Without contact with the original source, the
story of Judith becomes watered down and con-
fused. It's not uncommon to hear retellings in
which Judith fed Holofernes cheeses to make
him thirsty for wine—and thereby avoid having
to face the more earthy circumstance, in which it
was Holofernes' sexual passion for Judith that
made him drink too much. These poor retellings
obscure authentic legends as well. During the
saga of Jewish struggle for independence that
paralleled the rise of Rome, and when Yochanan
was High Priest, his daughter was desired by
the pagan ruler. It was she who fed this king's
lust with cheeses.

The Maccabean imagination is also preserved
in the domestic transformation of Hanukkah
rituals: a personalizing of the historical pomp
and propaganda. The eating of latkes is part of
the tradition of Hanukkah foods fried in oil,
where the oil is token of the Temple Menorah
legend. To be able to contain a memory of the
holy oil in the light-hearted spirit of latkes
sprinkled with sugar is no small imaginative

feat. It's not a demeaning of sacred tradition but an example of confidence in its endurance—a Maccabean confidence in transformation and renewal.

The First Book of Maccabees is an important history book, a witness to the drama of Jewish identity in a hostile world, and Hanukkah is a good time to study it. In itself, the book is not associated with the Hanukkah festival, yet contact with it reveals more of the festival's spirit than later versions. Among other historical insights, the book reminds us of the sympathies toward Greek culture among many Jews, including some Temple priests, which encouraged the Greek desire to convert *all* Jews to their "modern, progressive" ways. This element of the story is another level of nuance in Hanukkah's remembrance. Neither dwelling on this, nor isolating the usual passages recounting Maccabean military adventures (which are easily misunderstood out of the historical and literary context), I've chosen passages which illustrate the intensity of the Maccabean imagination.

The expansion of Jewish spirit leading to a Judean state in the second century B.C.E. created a crucible in which Judaism was able to confront the world on equal terms. That two-hundred-year experience of relative independence within the Greco-Roman world made a deeper impression on Jewish consciousness than any single

text can convey. The composer of First Maccabees recognized this, modeling his Hebrew
work on the biblical Books of Samuel. It's typical
of the Maccabean imagination to link itself with
tradition while freely creating new works; and
this is one reason Maccabean works were not allowed to actually replace tradition. The First
Book of Maccabees is too pretentious to be preserved as scripture, but it reveals the transform-
ative stage between biblical works and the work
of interpretation (as in Talmud and Midrash)
that nourished Judaism beyond the Maccabean
era.

Another feature of Maccabean times is the
evolution of personal prayer. The Temple was
central again, but it was also perceived that personal prayer was more than a substitute for
Temple rituals, as it had been during the
Babylonian exile. In personal prayer, it is selfhood that serves as the sacrificial animal. All of
this was known, but Maccabean boldness encouraged it further. It's as if suddenly it is not
strange to be aware that the whole universe is
the temple. And with that, Judaism was fully
revealed as a major world religion. It was able to
confront Hellenism openly, and it sustained the
Jewish martyrs in resisting the universal wave
of Greek "enlightenment." Countless Jews were
crucified for their religion, and many concepts
of sainthood evolved. The Books of Maccabees

record some of these developments, as do other apocryphal Jewish books. In the eyes of zealous Jews, Greek paganism worshipped the worst idolatry of all: selfhood.

The Book of Daniel expanded on much older legends of suffering and gave a deeper expression to Jewish consciousness as it confronted worldly power. Daniel exhibits the Maccabean imagination at its height of creative synthesis: the prophetic tradition redesigned for contemporary revelations. And with this came the unmistakable recognition that prophecy had ended centuries earlier (as a form of historical insight, passionate conscience, and visionary poetry—and not as crystal ball gazing, which remained an indulgence of fanatics). Daniel becomes the last book of the Hebrew Bible, as claims are made for undisciplined and idiosyncratic works that grow further and further away from the biblical tradition. Daniel is an authoritative spiritual text for Hanukkah, rooted in the already ancient Babylonian exile, its sophistication mirroring the depth of Maccabean imagination.

To understand Hanukkah it's necessary to go deeper, as the early rabbis did, into Jewish tradition. In the prophet Zechariah there's an image of the original menorah that Moses made, blazing eternally. It is this image that home

menorahs typify: their lights as much a remind-
er of days past as days to come. Judaism is
grounded in the universe of time, not the mys-
teries of space.

So the Hanukkah lights celebrate the richness
of Jewish memory and its perpetual renewal in
experience. The sections "A Blazing Fountain"
and "Illuminations" expand this awareness to
the original menorah: via history and imagination in "A Blazing Fountain" and via poetry and
prayer in "Illuminations." The Hanukkah
menorahs preserve the Maccabean imagination
by refining it into an image of an indestructible
Israel.

When the second Temple was desecrated by
the Seleucid Greek empire in 161 B.C.E., it was
the darkest day for Jews since the destruction of
their first Temple four hundred years earlier. It
toughened the resolve of the Maccabees—as the
Holocaust did for Israelis, and as Israel does
today for persecuted Jews in Russia. No present
or future event can atone for the Holocaust, including the state of Israel, and likewise Hanukkah is no solace for the Greek and Roman de-
structions and massacres of Jews. There is a way
in which Hanukkah reminds us that these cata-
clysms, like the Babylonian one, are submerged
in our collective conscience and unburied:
beyond the grasp of our comprehension.
Hanukkah honors this unembraceable memory
in the spirit of rededication to the original depth

of Jewish conscience—a refusal to turn away
from the world of experience.

The Maccabean triumph was in linking up
with the earlier "hanukkahs" of Jewish history,
in the thirteenth, the tenth, and the fifth centuries B.C.E., and the Hanukkah festival was in-
augurated at the recovery of the Temple in 164
B.C.E., many years before an independence was
won. So the military victories we remember are
overshadowed by a triumph of historical imagination. And the sources for Hanukkah in this
book unite all of these periods.

In order for the menorah symbolism to take
root in the Jewish heart, it was necessary to
neutralize and transform the dominant festival
of Greek pagan culture. The menorah lights
mark a deep resistance to the torchlight proces-
sions of the Hellenistic Dionysian festivals and
to the pagan bonfires of sun worship at the
winter solstice. In the same way, the menorah
and its lights symbolize a resistance to the dominant astrology: they are purified of any mystical relationship to star worship. Just as the as-
trological importance of the star at Christmas
was shorn of its pagan resonance in Christian
tradition, there were no stars in Hanukkah. The
lights of Hanukkah, while a profound protest
against pagan ceremony, burn the image of the
Temple menorah deeper into Jewish memory.

The transformation of fire-awe into the gent-

ler light of eternal renewal is typical of the imagination that preserves Hanukkah. The festival
was firmly anchored in Jewish tradition; its
spirit survives universalist crusades, and celebrates the right of all individuals to their own
character and identity. While the menorahs of
Hanukkah also reflect the joy of the Temple
Menorah light in the ancient Sukkot festival,
they signify something newer: an orientation to
reality in which imagination becomes a protest
against the "civilizing" forces of repression.

The spirit of this protest is a light one, tem-
pered by the kind of realism that Ecclesiastes
exhibits. Ecclesiastes is also a protest against the
overly material concerns and logic that find ex-
cuses for ignoring conscience. By resisting all
forms of sophisticated ignorance, it parallels the
Maccabean imagination in boldness. And like
the Book of Job, in which dogmatic wisdom is
incisively deflated, Ecclesiastes also demon-
strates a keen sense of irony.

Even before the Babylonian destruction and
exile, the catastrophes of Jewish history and the
redemptions were bound up together. The renewals come from the depths of tragedy. The
festival of Hanukkah, 164 years before the
Common Era, already commemorates this process and remains a remembrance of light growing in darkness—not a big, blinding light, but a
warm glow again in the darkest days of winter.

The Roman "new world" superseded the
Greek and was hardly the last one. Hanukkah re-
members something different in the realm of
Jewish nationhood: a return. And yet not a return to the past, but a transformation of it.
Today the central monument of modern Israel is
still connected to the Temple: a fragment of the
Western Wall still standing in Jerusalem, and
signifying an unbreakable integrity.

Out of the increasing persecution of Jews,
who hadn't had their independence for over
four hundred years, the vision revived and the
Maccabean revolt led to an independent Judean
state. It was as if an old cruse of oil was found to
rekindle the original spirit, because the Hanukkah festival commemorates the rededication of
the Temple: the link with a past that speaks of a
future. Zechariah the prophet spoke of that future centuries earlier, in the rebuilding of the
Temple and rekindling of the Menorah, and the
Hanukkah prayers speak of the renewals
throughout history—a form of "messianic
realism," as the notion of divine intervention
becomes imaginatively transformed into the
sense of personal participation in the nation's
renewal. The "Festival of Lights," as the Ro-
mans heard it called two thousand years ago,
continues the process of Jewish self-discovery.

THE BOOK OF JUDITH

A Modern Version

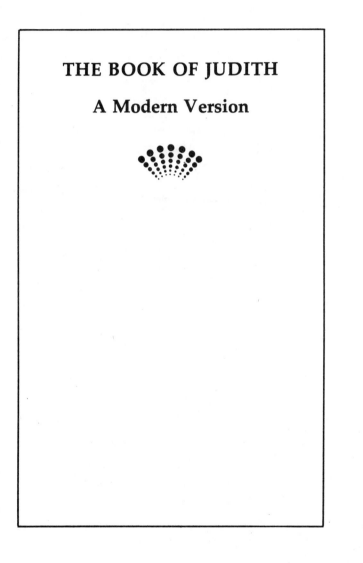

INTRODUCTION

The Book of Judith, one of the great poetic narratives of ancient Hebrew literature, was preserved in the Bible's Apocrypha. It was probably composed near the Maccabean Age and based on earlier legendary material. The book itself became a legend, after it was omitted from the Hebrew Bible, and it is rarely read in a Jewish context today. Where once the entire book was read in early synagogues to celebrate Hanukkah, it now is occasionally awarded brief passages in anthologies, and these selections are usually the blandest passages.

The Christian translations have always been popular. John Ruskin, in his Mornings in Florence, *characterized Judith as "the mightiest, purest, brightest type of high passion in severe womanhood offered to our human memory." But the best-known English translations of Judith, made in a non-Jewish context, do not dispel popular misconceptions about the book. For instance, the occasional Western tendency to be righteously shocked by violence (even to the extreme characterization of portions of Isaiah as "bloodthirsty") is similar to a fundamentalist reading of biblical Hebrew, where the metaphors and literary conventions are flattened and taken literally, missing the true poetry of*

17

the work. And as recently as 1977, a biblical scholar writing in the Anchor Bible continued to over-simplify the depth of Judith, assuming that it was omitted from the Jewish canon due to "later Jewish disapproval of the book's fanatical nationalism which, although quite understandable, in terms of the book's probable date of composition and histori-cal context, was nonetheless untempered by the ethical and moral considerations so characteristic of Judaism."

Judith is less refined than a legitimate biblical book, yet this "fanatical nationalism" has a meta-phorical sense as palpable as Judith's name, which simply means "Jewess" in Hebrew. By under-valuing its literary sophistication, the ethical in-tegrity of Judith will also be missed, especially when compared to later, more didactic works. One of the fierce charges leveled against Jews by early Chris-tians was that their "nationalism" was an "evil genius" that negated the universalism of Christian faith (echoed by the Gnostic scholar G. R. S. Mead in Fragments of a Faith Forgotten). *In fact, the text of Judith makes it clear that the Jews do not look for victory but merely survival: the victory celebration in the book is a literary antidote to the cruel intentions of the enemy. It is as obvious a conventional exaggeration as the victory over Haman in the Book of Esther. Likewise, the popular imagery of war, heroism, and piety is highly stylized—the real passion in this poetry lies elsewhere.*

As in most Jewish writing, when vengeance is invoked it is as a mirror image for the attacker's own self-destruction, a hope that he will be trapped by his own destructive plans. Judith's beauty was an instrument of truth allowing Holofernes and the inflated self-pride of the worldly power he represented to fall on its own face.

Another major misconception of the Book of Judith arises from translating as if it were prose fiction. Judith is written in a highly poeticized form of narrative which loses its texture in a prose translation. For instance, one of the main poetic features is frequent use of biblical quotations, phrases, and parallels to deepen the rhythm and harmonics of the narrative. In fact, the narration is often secondary to the immediate feelings these echoes arouse. And then there are the large sections of formal poetry themselves: psalms, prayers, songs, and invocations. There is also the steady echo of biblical poetry in the historical tone throughout the book; and the Victorian critic Ruskin was able to recognize Judith as "epic poetry" in the context of a deep literary perspective. In modern terms especially, this "story" is closer to poetry than fiction, and I have adapted it accordingly.

Just as the eleventh chapter of Daniel is probably a work of the Maccabean Age, Judith also portrays its own times in an older historical focus. There are many reasons for this convention, literary and otherwise. One is the obvious need to disguise contemporary political criticism—the "King

Nebuchadnezzar" of *Judith is probably the same
Greek-Seleucid Antiochus as in the eleventh chapter of Daniel. It was natural to use the Babylonian
Nebuchadnezzar as an archetype because the Jewish
sense of cultural renaissance dated back to the return
from Babylonian exile. The events surrounding the
first destruction of the Temple and the Exile are archetypal for the Maccabean "Hanukkah": the rededication of Temple and nation. The conventions
of "prophetic history" were transparent to contemporary Jews, a source of both political satire and
religious inspiration.*

*It has always been a literary convention to pro-
ject criticism of the present back into remote
history—in Shakespeare no less than in the early
Greek dramatists. It is probable that the Hebrew
composer of Judith was familiar with Greek writing.
Judith as a type of heroine would have been an accepted convention for audiences contemporary with
Sophocles—and the legend of Judith probably
originated in Israel around that time (400 B.C.E.).
But just as Euripides in Greece, only a few years
later, reflected the eclipse of the days of individual
heroes, the final composer of Judith, writing at a
later date, adapted the heroic convention into the
Jewish tradition by "modernizing" it. He fleshed
out its monotheistic focus, deepened by a paralleling of biblical books, and made it something more
than a drama or romance: a work of prophetic history. The poignancy of the allusion to the rededica-*

tion (the "hanukkah") of the Temple in chapter
four of Judith would not be lost on a Maccabean
ear.

So when we rediscover that the Book of Judith
was read in the early synagogue on Hanukkah, it
seems appropriate. A passionate poetic narrative,
the Book of Judith is motivated by intense outrage at
the arrogance of the pagan Greek imperialism. This
rage is sublimated into the presentation of a beautiful woman who is Judaism itself: religious but at the
same time acutely oriented to reality. Her sublime
physicality, rooted in domestic happiness and a
sense of communal responsibility, contrasts with
the inflated pride of the pagans. No angels or miracles are employed in this victory—justice is done as
the enemy does himself in, a victim of his own arrogance.

It is just as natural to rediscover that the necessity for Judith to carry cheeses with her into the
pagan camp, to keep kosher with a dairy diet (and,
as well, to further heighten the irony of Holofernes'
"banquet plan") is behind the long tradition of eating dairy dishes such as cheese pancakes and latkes
at Hanukkah. We do not do it as a heavy ritual, but
rather in a buoyant spirit. It is the same spirit that
permeates the Book of Judith, a heady sense of relief
at having survived.

The psalm near the end of the Book of Judith contains more of the Maccabean spirit than any form of
narrative that has come down to us. It is a narrative

poem suffused with the sense of individual prayer —history made personal —that dates back to the Exile in Babylon, where prayer substituted for Temple. rituals. Now the Temple was a reality again, and the passion of prayer, conveyed by poetry, is central to the narrative of Judith. Prayer, like poetry, is as old as the hills, but the Book of Judith preserves a renewed sense of personal prayer based in experience.

THE BOOK OF JUDITH

*In the twelfth year of Nebuchadnezzar's reign he began
to plan a war against the powerful nation of the Medes.
When Nebuchadnezzar called on smaller nations to join
him as allies they refused, unafraid, sensing his power
was overplayed. He was severely embarrassed, and
when he later defeated the Medes he planned retribution.*

*Holofernes, the Assyrian army's commander-in-chief,
put together a huge expeditionary force, with over a
hundred and twenty thousand foot soldiers alone, and
marched out of Nineveh toward Damascus, intent on destroying all resistance. The method was simple: wipe out
local religions and cultures. After devastating various
nations, leveling towns across Mesopotamia and Arabia,
"butchering all who resisted," the Assyrian approaches
Damascus.*

And he surrounded the Arabs
burning their tents, looting their flocks
then came down into the plain of Damascus
it was during the wheat harvest and he set fire
to the crops, the fields were ablaze
herds destroyed, villages ransacked
and all the young men skewered on the sword

Panic gripped the coast
in Sidon, in Tyre
in Sur, Akko, Jamnia

Ashdod and Ashkelon lived in terror
they sent their highest messengers
begging peace: "We are here as servants
of the great Nebuchadnezzar, to lie at your feet
do with us what you like
the doors of our warehouses stand open
our flocks, our herds are under your command
every farm and field of wheat
lies at your feet
use them as you like
our cities and every citizen in them only wonder
what they can do for you, what's your pleasure"
these were their exact words to Holofernes
then he descended the coast and garrisoned the
          cities
where he made allies, chose conscripts
and received a hero's welcome
with garlands, tambourines, and dancing in
          celebration
meanwhile his army set fire to border villages
destroying claims to independent boundaries
he cut down all their groves of sacred trees
demolished all their pagan shrines
defiled every god they'd clung to
so it would be realistic for them to turn
to Nebuchadnezzar as a god
uniting nations under his worldly power
transcending all their local languages

Holofernes approached the plain of Jezreel near
          Dothan

sages to Jerusalem he was astonished. He asked his loca
allies what gave this people the nerve to resist, and h
was told it was faith in their God, demonstrated by a long
history of survival. The Assyrian and his generals were
furious when they heard this unrealistic answer, since
Nebuchadnezzar obviously deserved to be recognized as
the only god: his power and strength were visibly evi-
dent.

So Holofernes gave orders to wipe out this people. And
the local allies advised a siege of the strategic city guard-
ing the best route to Jerusalem. This way, the strategic
mountain positions of the Jews were useless, and the As-
syrians wouldn't lose a single soldier in battle.

After thirty-four days, Bethulia ran out of water.
People were fainting in the streets. The town council ac-
cused the leaders of a grave error in not begging peace
like other peoples. They would rather be alive as slaves
than watch their children die. As a last resort, one leader
appealed for holding out five more days; if nothing
changed by then, he would advise surrender.

Judith, beautiful and devout, a widow still in mourn-
ing, visited the leaders and accused them differently.
Who were they to set a time limit for God? They were
actually negating their faith by setting conditions for
miracles. But Judith declines to pray for rain when she is
asked. When she does pray, in the psalm beginning chap-
ter nine, it is for strength and guidance in a plan of realis-
tic action. The activity of prayer itself is symbolically
correlated to responsible initiative.

Then Judith kneeled
put her face in the dust
stripped to the sackcloth she wore
        underneath—
just at the moment the evening incense offering
wafted to the Temple ceiling in Jerusalem—

where Judean mountains begin to be seen
he pitched camp between Geba and Beth Shear
staying there at least a month to regroup
and gather supplies for his army

By now the Jews in Judea had heard about
      Holofernes
commander-in-chief of the Assyrian army
under King Nebuchadnezzar, and how tith
      nations
looting their sacred shrines, then leveling them
they were quite scared, near despair for
      Jerusalem
place of their one God's temple
they had hardly returned from exile
only recently had rededicated the devastated
      Temple
cleaning the altar, restoring the vessels
reunited in their land

              (2:26–28; 3; 4:1–3)

*Unlike the surrender pleas of their neighbors, the orders
from Jerusalem were to occupy the mountaintops and
passages, buying time for the protection of Jerusalem.
The Jews were in no position to defend their country
militarily, but they could hope to appear not worth the
trouble of subduing. And they could pray for survival. It
wasn't a victory they prayed for, but to be spared a mas-
sacre and cultural annihilation.*

   When Holofernes heard that Jews had closed the pas-

cupped her face in her hands
and spoke
her words rising outspoken
from her heart to the open sky
an offering, a prayer:

"Lord, God of my fathers
of Simon in whose hand you put a sword
to reward the strangers
who stripped off a young girl's dress to her
        shame
bared the innocence between her thighs
to her deep confusion
and forced into her womb
raped her in shock
to demean and disgrace her

For you have said in the Torah
this is an outrage
and you allowed these violators to be surprised
in their beds of deceit
the sheets stripped off them
their beds blushing with shame:
stained with their blood

For the lords among these strangers
you allowed equal treatment with their slaves:
slain on their thrones
their servants in their arms
their wives and daughters allowed to be spared:
captured and dispersed

Their possessions fell into the hands
of the sons you loved
for they listened to you
and were outraged
at the demeaning of a sister's blood
they called on you for help
and you listened
Lord, my Lord
now hear this widow's selfless words
you gave shape to the past
and beneath what is happening now
is your supportive hand
you have thought about the future
and those thoughts live as men and women
'Here we are!' they say
your thoughts are alive in the present
and you've cleared paths for them
into the future

Look, here we are, exposed to the Assyrians
parading their well-oiled muscle
preening in the mirrors of their polished shields
bullying the hills with their herds of infantry
vanity worn on their sleeves: tin armor
their spears thrusting forward
their trust in their legs and horses
their pride in the naked tips of their arrows
their hope in thoughts of total domination—
so locked in the embrace of themselves
they can't know you are Lord over all
fierce in your shattering of wars themselves

great armies of the past are dust in your
        presence
they were lords in their own eyes as they
        marched on blindly
but there is only one 'Lord'

Lord, crush their violence
break their thoughts to bits in your anger
at their shameless threats of power
they want to force their way into your sanctuary
to cut off the ancient horn on your altar
to strip bare the ark
in which you are held holy
to demean your spirit with swords of tin and
        iron
to debase your name

Look at the arrogance of their thoughts
cut them off in outrage
bow their heads in shame
sweep a mental sword through their minds

Put your sword in the hand of a widow
give me the presence of mind
to overpower them with pointed speech
in the sheath of an alluring voice
to confuse them with an inner truth
shaping words of steel
to slay 'equally' masters with their slaves
servant and petty lord
while they are inflated by selfish desire

while they are charmed by feminine lips
while they are caught in their self-deception
shatter their pride
disperse their power
by a woman's hand

Your force is not visible in numbers and armor
does not stand at attention before men of war
your power is indivisible and disarms violence
and you are a Lord to the powerless
help to the oppressed
support to the weak, refuge to the humble
a sudden rescue, a saviour to the lost
warmth in the coldest despair
light in the most hopeless eyes

Please hear me, God of my father
Lord of Israel's heritage
Master of the universe, Creator of earth and sky
King of all creation
hear my psalm

Let my words be lies they cannot hear
sharpen my tongue with charm
my lips irresistable
mirroring their inner deceit
which stares back into their surprised faces
as my words cut deep
like a sudden knife
into those with cruel plans
against our heart, against your spirit

and the Temple of your spirit
the mountain of Zion
the house of your children
in Jerusalem, and let the whole nation
all nations
suddenly understand
that you are Lord and God and King
above all force and power

and Israel stands
by your shield."

(Chapter 9)

Judith's prayer was over
she rose from the ground
called to her maid
and in the house removed the sackcloth
and widow's dress, then bathed
in creams and expensive perfumes
and did her hair
crowned with a subtle tiara
and put on her most attractive dress
not worn since her husband Manasseh died
and before that only on joyous occasions—
slender sandals adorned her feet
brightened by jeweled anklets
bracelets and rings on her arms and fingers
earrings and pins and other jewelry

making up such a beautiful picture
that any man or woman's head would turn—
she gave her maid flasks of oil and a skin of
        wine
fig cakes and dried fruit
a bag filled with barley cakes and roasted grains
cheeses
and loaves of sweetest challah
then carefully wrapped her own dishes
and koshered pottery
also for her maid to carry . . .

They kept walking straight across the valley
until sighted by Assyrian advance troops
who seized Judith, interrogated her
"Where do you come from?
What people do you belong to?
Where are you going?"
"I'm a daughter of Hebrews
but I'm escaping from them
because they are fodder for you
to be devoured as simply as grain in a bowl
I want to be taken to Holofernes your Lord
I can report the truth to him
I want to show him the simplest way
to take over the mountains and approaches
surrounding this country
without losing a single man
subduing it without so much as a bruise"

As these men listened to her well-chosen words
they saw the noble beauty in Judith's face
and (coupled with her directness) they were
      overwhelmed
by such physical elegance in a woman
"You have saved your life
not hesitating to come directly
into the presence of our lord
you will be taken straight to his tent
and we will announce you to him—
have no fear in your heart
when you are in his presence
because when you tell him what you told us
he will treat you with deep respect"
a detachment of a hundred men escorted the
      two women

So Judith and her maid came safely
to the tent of Holofernes—
but not without causing a stir in the whole camp
the news was buzzing from tent to tent
and while Judith waited outside the
      commander's tent
a crowd gathered around her
amazed at her beauty
this was the first they'd seen of an Israelite
and coupled with what they'd heard
they were amazed at the presence of this people
as their curiosity fed on her grace
"Who can despise a people with women like
      this?"

they were saying
"We'll have to wipe out this entire race
every last one of them
just as we were told to do
because any that survive will probably outwit
just about anyone in the world—
moved simply by the agony of loss
of such grace and beauty
to bring our world to its knees
as surely as a disarmed suitor"

Then Holofernes' personal guards came out
to escort Judith into the tent
where he was resting on his bed
under the fine gauze mosquito-net
that was a precious, royal canopy
purple interwoven with fine strands of gold
studded with emeralds
and many other gems: as stunning as a crown

When Judith was announced he came out
silver lamps carried by servants leading the way
into the front part of the tent
and he saw her standing there and was amazed
at so beautiful a face
she bowed touching her face to the ground
in homage, but his servants quickly lifted her up
"Feel at ease, woman"
Holofernes was saying
"Have no fear in your heart
I've never hurt anyone who made the choice

to serve Nebuchadnezzar, king of this world
I didn't choose to raise a spear
against your people in the hills
they've brought me here themselves
insulting me by taking us lightly
now tell me why you've escaped from them
to join us—but first, be at ease
you have saved your life
take heart, you've found a new life here
free of fear
no one can threaten you tonight or any other
    night
you'll learn what it is to be at ease in your life
to be an equal and treated as well
as any servant of my Lord, King
    Nebuchadnezzar . . .

*Judith's speech before Holofernes, like other untranslated
passages in the following portion, is inferred.*

Judith's words enchanted Holofernes
they were so well-measured
all his attendants were amazed at such wisdom
"There isn't a woman in the whole world
to match this fresh intelligence
lighting up the beauty of her face"
And above the buzzing Holofernes said to her
"God has done well
to bring you in advance of his people
into our hands, strengthening us
so we may bring a just destruction

to those so blind as to take us lightly
having insulted my lord by refusing to kneel—
your God will right their wrongs himself
if you do as you've said
for your words are well-chosen
and you are a beautiful woman
your God shall live and be treated as my god
as you will live in the palace
of King Nebuchadnezzar, so your fame
may spread through the whole world."

The fourth day after Judith arrived
Holofernes planned a private feast
bypassing the invitations most banquets
    require
to all the officers, and he called in Bagoas
his head eunuch who was taking charge of
    Judith
"Talk to the Hebrew woman
persuade her to join us for a feast
it's disgraceful not to know her better
everyone will laugh at us for not courting
such a beautiful woman while she's here"

When Bagoas came to Judith he was all flattery
"Have no fear fair lady
of my lord, and he will be honored
if you will come into his presence
to drink wine and be his guest

at an intimate feast
and be a chosen daughter of Assyria
beginning to live today
like a daughter in the House of
        Nebuchadnezzar"
Judith was ready with an answer
"And who am I to refuse my lord?
I desire only to be of service
pleasing him will make me happy today
and will always be
something I will cherish until the day I die"

And so she began to dress
in the fine clothes she had brought
in the cosmetics, jewelry and alluring perfume
and in gentle ceremony she sent her maid ahead
to lay the soft fleeces Bagoas lent to her
on the floor in Holofernes' tent
where she would eat and then lean back

When Judith came in and Holofernes saw her
leaning back on her fleeces
his heart was overwhelmed
and his mind filled with desire
lit by a wish to sleep with her
from the first time he saw her
in fact for these four days he'd been searching
for a way to seduce her
and so he was saying "Drink
relax and let yourself go with us"
"I'd love to, my lord

today I've found a reason to live
beyond anything I've dreamed of since I was
        born"

Facing him, Judith ate and drank
the food her maid had brought and prepared
and Holofernes having accepted her reason
for being true to her God's rituals
was disarmed at her acceptance of him
and so excited at the thought of having her
he drank to his heart's content
until he'd poured out more wine in one night
than he'd drank of anything in a day
since he was born

Now it was getting late and the staff
were leaving, tipsy, but quickly, as if they knew
Bagoas rolled down the outside tent flap
then dismissed the servants
(natural enough since they were exhausted)
and they went straight to sleep
leaving Judith alone with Holofernes
who had wound up sprawling on his bed
his head swimming in wine

Earlier, on the way to the feast
Judith asked her maid not to leave
if dismissed later, but to wait outside the
        bedroom
just as she did on previous mornings
since now everyone expected her early rising

and going out for ritual prayers
she had even reminded Bagoas and now
all had gone
not a soul important or unimportant
was left in the bedroom
Judith stood by Holofernes' bed
a silent prayer in her heart:

"Lord, my God, source of all power
have mercy on me for what my hands must do
for Jerusalem to be a living example
of trust in your covenant
now is the time to renew our heritage
give my plan life
to surprise the enemies
to bring them to their knees
who've risen up all around us
great herds coming to devour us"

Her hand reached up
for Holofernes' well-honed sword
hanging on the front bedpost
slung there in its jeweled scabbard
then, standing directly over him, swiftly
her left hand seized hold of his hair
"Make me steel, Lord, God of Israel—today"
as with all her strength she struck
at the nape of his neck, fiercely
and again—twice—and she pulled
his head from him
then rolled the severed body from the bed

and tore down the royal canopy
from the bedposts

A moment later she stepped out from the
        bedroom
and gave the head, wrapped in the canopy, to
        her maid
who put it in the sack she carried
with all of Judith's food and vessels

The two women walked out together
just as they usually did for prayer
they passed through the camp
walked straight across the valley
climbed the mountain to Bethulia
and approached the city gates.

                              (10:1–5, 11–23;
                              11:1–4, 20–23;
                              12:10–20; 13:1–10)

Chapter fourteen and the beginning of chapter fifteen describe Judith's reception in Bethulia, the rout of the Assyrians, and the victory celebration. A subplot is concluded, in which Achior, a neighbor who respected the Jews, identifies Holofernes' head, then asks to be circumcised and is "incorporated in the House of Israel forever." The book ends with the arrival in Jerusalem, and then a brief description of Judith's later life and death.

All the women of Israel come out to see her
on the way to Jerusalem
flushed with the victory they shared
of faith over power
grace and daring over brute force
some began a dance in celebration
Judith was carrying palm branches in her arms
passing them to the women around her
they were all garlanding themselves with olive
Judith at the head of the procession
to Jerusalem, leading the women who were
        dancing
and the men of Israel who were following
dressed in their armor and garlands
songs and psalms from their lips
lightening the feet of the dancers

Then Judith began this psalm of thanksgiving
and all the people joined her, repeating the lines
the psalm of a Jewess echoed by Israel:

"Strike a beat for my God with tambourines
ringing cymbals lift a song to the Lord
a new psalm rise from a fresh page of history
inspired with his name
call on him for inspiration
My Lord is the God who crushes war
in the midst of the warmonger's camp

Jerusalem is pitched like a tent
in the camp of Israel

and here he has delivered me
from the grasping hands of my enemy

The Assyrian swarmed over the mountains in
    the north
with tens of thousands in armor
gleaming in purple and gold
hordes of infantry like rivers
flooding the valleys
an avalanche of horsemen
pouring down on the plains
my borders would be flames he said
my young men skewered on swords
infants flung to the ground
children seized for slaves
and my daughters for whores

But the Lord God has let them be outwitted
with a woman's hand
their hero fell
and not a young man's hand touched him
not the sons of warrior giants
neither a Goliath nor David
but Judith, daughter of Merari
stopped him in his tracks
paralyzed his brutal power
with the beauty of her face

And instead of fame for fleeting glamor
she is held in honor
because she didn't think of herself

but faced disaster head-on
firmly on the open path, God's way

She put aside her widow's dress
to save the honor of the living
those oppressed in Israel
she anointed her face with perfume
bound her hair beneath a delicate headband
and put on attractive linen to lure him
but only to his own undoing
her slender sandal imprisoning his eye
her beauty taking his heart captive
for the sword to cut through his neck

Persians shivered at her boldness
and Medes shuddered in terror

My humble people were suddenly raising their
        voices
my weak little nation was shouting with joy
while the enemy, shocked, ran off in fear
they panicked as my people danced in the
        streets
the sons of mere women pierced their lines
mamas' boys chased them as they ran
willy-nilly they ran away like brave sons of
        eunuchs

Their battle lines were erased
like lines in the sand
under the pursuing boots of Israel

I will sing a new psalm to my God
Lord, you are great, you are our glory
your strength so marvelously deep,
        unconquerable
may all your creation recognize you
because you allowed everything here
to be
you said the word and we're here
and the breath behind it is our air
your spirit breathes the form of all things
it opens our ears
no one can resist your voice
the message of creation is always there

Mountains may fall into the sea
and seas crack open like a broken glass of water
rocks may melt like wax
but for those who live in awe of you
your presence is a steady candle
glowing warmth and a guide to safety
all the burning sacrifices are quickly mere
        fragrance
all the fat of sacrificial lambs a brief aroma
compared to one person in awe of you
whose strength is always there

All nations who come to destroy my people
beware of justice, you will disappear
your peoples will see a day of judgment
before God, My Lord
but all they will know is the fire in their hearts

sparked by inflated pride
a pain that will always burn there
as they are confined in the room of their minds:
their flesh will be consumed in it
and given to worms."

(15:12–14; 16:1–17)

from FIRST BOOK OF
MACCABEES

INTRODUCTION

The First Book of Maccabees was written in Hebrew, incorporating some earlier Hebrew historical records. It is a polished literary work by a single author. Its style is straightforward, the author subtly effacing his personal identity behind a vivid and objective narrative—but in the appropriate places he steps into the picture with bold editorial enthusiasm, just often enough to keep the reader aware of the partisan Jewish context. The book is not wholly narrative but includes portions of passionate poetry and prayer.

We've lost the original Hebrew manuscript. But a Jewish translation into Greek was made very soon after it was written, for use by the large Jewish population living in Egypt and other Hellenistic cultures, including Judea itself. As these Jewish communities were transformed in character by the Roman rise to power and Jewish Greek died out, the Greek version was kept intact by the early Christian church, which included the first two Books of Maccabees in their version of the Old Testament.

In place of the original Hebrew text, the legend of the Maccabees was kept alive among Jews in the form of parochial Hebrew paraphrases and poems, such as the medieval Scroll of Antiochus. However, these later versions do not approach the original book in depth, range, style, or authenticity, and their use has largely died out in modern times. I have gone back to the original book, aided by the remarkable Hebrew version (a translation from the Greek back into Hebrew, as well as a reconstruction of the original Hebrew) of Abraham Kahana, first published in Jerusalem in 1931. There are earlier Hebrew versions as well, including a popular nineteenth-century version, but Kahana's is an improvement and is vastly superior to any English translation. It was recently reprinted, in 1969, in a two-volume edition of Ha-Sefarim Ha-Hitzonim.

There have been countless English translations, predating the King James Version of the Bible on up to the most recent Bible translations in England and America. There is also a Jewish translation, printed en face *with the original Greek translation, in the series of books called "Jewish Apocryphal Literature." The problem with all of these translations, beyond the usual one of inferior literary quality, is that the original Hebrew version resonates with allusions, phrases, images, and stylistic echoes of the Hebrew Bible—and this context is obscured in translation from the Greek text.*

Like the Book of Judith, the First Book of Maccabees keeps within the limits of natural experience—no direct supernatural miracles are performed. Though God's presence is felt in the unfolding of events, it is in terms of the faith men hold in him. This faith is especially emphasized because of the pressure for its destruction or assimilation that comes from the Hellenized Greek empire. The First Book of Maccabees tells the story of Jewish resistance to the Greeks and then chronicles the Maccabean campaigns and the Hasmonean dynasty that comes to power in Judea. The festival of Hanukkah is born during the Maccabean Era, sustained through later generations and, in the process of becoming established beyond its limitations of time and place, is transformed.

The seeds of Hanukkah's ultimate transformation into a major holiday may be found in the scattered psalms and prayers quoted by the author of First Maccabees, and attributed to Mattathias or Judah. In my versions of these psalms, as well as brief prose passages, I have concentrated on the broader sense of the Hanukkah festival and not just its debt to the exploits of Mattathias the Priest and his sons, including Judah Maccabee. The latter are important and inspiring, but I believe they have come to be distorted in historical context just because they are too legendary for the secularized Jew or Christian (who, after all, glorified the Maccabean legend in Western culture) —those wishing to draw their identity from a romantic source.

The term "hanukkah," which means "dedication" in Hebrew, was in use long before the Maccabean Era. In his edition of The Haphtoroth *(London, 1966), Mendel Hirsch describes the usage of the Hanukkah haftorah from the prophet Zechariah: "On the Festival of the fourth chanuka,*

*the chanuka of the Maccabees, the reading from the
Prophets on Sabbath brings to our minds the remembrance of the third, that of Zerubbabel." This
larger historical perspective imbued the celebration
of Hanukkah with its timeless character, even in the
midst of finite events, and anchored it in the Jewish
collective consciousness which the modern Jewish
philosopher, Mordecai Kaplan, calls "awareness
of the unchanging character of the relationship
between God and Israel."*

*When the Temple was destroyed again in the year
70 C.E., the festival of Hanukkah survived, just as
the lighting of menorahs in homes already began a
transformation of Temple ritual into more personal
observance. The suspension of sacrificial rites in the
Temple and the ancient priesthood did not diminish
faith—the continuity in Jewish practice was main-
tained as the biblical descriptions of Temple ritual
became part of the daily and festival liturgy. These
biblical readings are not only authentic roots of
Judaism, they are manifestations of the same
spiritual world that we touch today in the form of
study, prayer, and interpretation. Every man and
woman becomes as central as a temple; prayer and
awareness long ago superseded the necessity of
priests and ceremonial rituals on a priestly altar.
Likewise, our awareness of the historical roots of
Hanukkah deepens our sense of its significance.*

*Today, the long historical consciousness of survi-
val and renewal is preserved in the new state of Israel. The true spirit of Hanukkah is not in the goal*

of a reestablished state, but in the sense of renewal itself. The joy in the festival is not in military victory, but in the integrity of resistance. The Maccabees resisted the worldwide wave of Greek Hellenism that suppressed all local religions. Israel and Rome were the only nations to withstand it—Rome by might, Israel by spirit. First Maccabees tells the story of that resistance in its record of physical struggles with insensitive worldly power. And the Jewish spirit that survives is still at home in the physical world of experience.

from FIRST BOOK OF MACCABEES

Then the king published a law that made all the subjects of his empire one people. They were to abandon local laws, tied to outmoded cultures and religions. The pagan nations accepted this modernization, converting to the king's religion and sacrificing to its idols. Many Jews did the same, worshipping idols and eagerly denouncing the sabbath.

Then the king wrote to Jerusalem and all towns in Judea outlawing Jewish practice: Temple rituals were banned, sabbaths and festivals were to be renounced. The Jews were to practice paganism and defile their Temple, depose their priests, build altars to the Greek gods, make local temples and fill them with idols, sacrifice pigs, and leave their sons uncircumcised. They were to prostitute themselves, abandon their Torah, and forget their Jewish customs. Anyone breaking the new law would be executed.

(1:41–50)

On the 25th of Kislev, 146th year of the Seleucid-Babylonian Era (168 B.C.E.): *desolation*—the idols of the Olympian Zeus were erected in the Temple and, on the altar, unutterable desecration. Then pagan altars were built in towns all over Judea; sacrifices were made in town squares and "holy" incense burned in the streets. Books of the Torah were ripped to pieces and burned also. For anyone possessing these books or caught practicing any Jewish custom: the death sentence.

Month after month, Jews were denounced and brutally treated by the Greek accomplices, who took power in all the cities. And on the twenty-fifth of each month they made pagan sacrifices in the Lord's Temple. They were zealous for the new laws, executing women who were found with circumcised babies. The baby clung to its mother's breast as she was crucified or thrown from the walls or cliffs. The husbands and family were also crucified, along with those attending the circumcision.

There were many Israelites with enough inner strength to resist the laws. They would rather have died than prostitute Israel's covenant. And they were executed. Israel lived in a reign of terror—there was no help.

(1:54–64)

Mattathias was a priest from Jerusalem who had moved to the village of Modin, escaping Jerusalem's devastation. He is the father of Judah Maccabee and Judah's brothers John, Simon, Eliezer, and Jonathan. This psalm is attributed to him, and its feeling adds motivation to the description of the first act of Jewish resistance that follows: Mattathias refuses to offer a sacrifice to the Greek-Seleucid king, is driven to kill an apostate collaborator together with the king's officer, pulls down the pagan altar, and takes to the hills and mountains with his sons. The armed revolt is now a reality. But first—this psalm of Jewish identity. In it, the image of a beautiful, free woman (heightening the typically feminine imagery of Jerusalem) is parallel to imagery in the Book of Judith.

A Psalm of Mattathias

Did I have to be born
raised to be a witness
to Jerusalem taken like a whore

my people massacred in spirit
sitting propped up like dead men
watching their city fall as if at a play

a foreign theater
at which they do not understand the language
but see their Temple stripped before their eyes

naked in the hands of enemies
and the audience disrobed: by the eyes
blind to their shame

sitting at a dumbshow
as if shy before the beauty
of their heritage

the very vessels
of the House
of Israel

paraded before them
in the hands of thieves
carried off into dark exile

and Israel watches
as her babes are killed in their mother's arms
her young men slain over their books

in her streets and in her squares
again the curtain rises
another nation plays the conqueror

like many have done before it
having their way with her
leaving her stripped of personal possessions

she was a beautiful free woman
that now is left a slave
look, open your eyes

the Temple is empty
that was the vision of beauty
the glory in our lives

the spirit ripped from our chests—
do we just lean back
and go on living?

(2:7–13)

*When Mattathias is ready to die, now a hero to Israel, he
speaks to his sons about the need to continue the armed
resistance. Within this speech is the short psalm that follows, an echo of earlier biblical psalms.*

A Psalm of Mattathias

There is no need for fear
of men dressed in threats of power
all their successes are masks

that will fade like words in a gust of wind
and though one walks as if he wears a crown
in a show of pride—the whole performance
    collapses

in an instant: one last breath
and his body crowns the dunghill
and his words have turned to worms

today he shines on everyone's tongue
tomorrow no one has heard of him
he's vanished quickly as a winter sunset

gone—turned back into dust
all his schemes turned back
into nothing

but you, my children, take hold of your lives
by a stronger hand
by the deep strength in Torah

your hearts unsinkable vessels
bearing its words: sustenance
for a day beyond mere dreams of success

it will bring you into the future
it will bring you courage
worn as surely as a crown.

                    (2:62–64)

This psalm is not meant to sound entirely like a spontaneous composition, but an echo of an ancient biblical psalm that parallels the earlier Babylonian destruction and exile. It is quoted as a prayer by Judah and his people as they prepare for the battle. Like the earlier psalms of Mattathias, it heightens the scene and deepens the historical perspective. It also describes the contemporary Jerusalem situation in passionate contrast to the matter-of-factness of the historical narrative.

A Psalm of Judah

Jerusalem was a desert
empty of its spirit
none of her children were left

who had been signs of life
and none would go in
even Jerusalem air so pure

seemed choked with dust
the spirit that once breathed deeply
beheaded

the Temple quiet as a graveyard
walked upon by foreigners
as if it were grass

strangers were sleeping in the citadel
another desolate renovation
by pagans

Jacob awoke in a nightmare
and his children had gone
joy had abandoned him

flute and lyre
pipe and zither
had ceased.

(3:45)

After they had prayed, "having unrolled the Torah scrolls, finding in words the inspiration which pagans implored from idols" (3:48), the battle trumpets sounded.

Then Judah appointed officers to form an army from the people according to biblical practice: leaders for squads of ten, for groups of fifty, of a hundred, of a thousand. As it is also written in the Torah, Judah ordered all men home who were still building their houses, or engaged to be married, or had planted vineyards, or held objections of any kind to fighting.

The rebel army marched out to take up position south of Emmaus. There Judah told them, "Be prepared to fight, to show the conscience you are made of. At dawn we'll attack the pagans who have joined forces only to destroy Jews and wipe out our home in Jerusalem. It is better to die in open defense than watch the destruction of our nation and Temple like bystanders. But we are ready for whatever happens, our nation's conscience is open to God's will."

(3:55–60)

The next day, as Judah surveys the battlefield (his men outnumbered by sixty-five thousand to ten thousand— Second Maccabees suggests an even larger disparity), he offers this psalm, which is an early instance of a prayer that begins with the same words used to preface benedic-

tions in Jewish life: Barukh Atah Adonai . . . *This is not a request for vengeance, but a prayer for the strength of a deeper motivation. In many ways it is like Judith's psalms—she invoked the Jewish heritage just as Judah does, and rather than asking for supernatural physical power or intervention, they both pray for a strength and inspiration that will break the enemy's spirit. The psalms are examples of personal prayer in the communal tradition.*

The Maccabean victory in this battle made it possible for Judah to enter Jerusalem and inaugurate the Hanukkah, which will be described shortly.

A Psalm of Judah

When Judah saw how huge the enemy expedition was, he prayed:

You are deeply felt
Lord beyond lords
Israel's strength is with you

who broke the spirit of warriors
crushing their plans along with their violent
        hero
by the hand of David, your servant

and the power of the Philistine army was
        dismantled
falling into the hand
of Jonathan, son of Saul—

in the same way, dismay this army
by the hand of Israel
humble their pride in superior number and
    horses

let their hearts be crushed by shame
let them be struck by panic
their arrogance melt away

let them quake in their boots
and run away in fear of destruction
by a people who love you

and let all who feel the power
behind your name which is a shield
feel like singing psalms to you.

(4:30–33)

The following passage describes the inauguration of Hanukkah as a result of the joy in returning to Jerusalem and the Temple—of having resisted and survived— paralleling the joy of the ancient Sukkot festival. The emotion of the occasion is recreated by contrasting the joy with the sense of shock in suddenly being confronted with the desolate Temple. (Historical parallels include the mingled "weeping and joy" at the dedication of the altar in Ezra's time, centuries earlier.)

Now Judah and his brothers came to realize there was time to go up to the Temple. They'd pushed the enemy out, now it was theirs. The Temple was theirs again, and one of the brothers said, "We can put down our armor and begin to restore the sanctuary, and then we'll rededicate it."

The entire army assembled at the foot of Mount Zion, and then they went up. The enemy had fled to its bunker in the citadel. The Jewish army saw their Temple—it was deserted, a desert, utter desecration. The altar was in pieces and smeared with dirt. The gates to the holy sanctuary had been torn down and burned. The prayer courts were overgrown with weeds— image of an abandoned ruin: where they had lived, yesterday, the vision living within them. The inner chambers were rubble. The ark sheer desolation. A home stripped naked to wind and rain, their vision disfigured, looted by blind men.

Stunned, they held themselves in their own arms, as if there were babies in their arms, as if their hearts would fall out of their chests. They sobbed like mothers who had lost their children. Some broke out in wails, some knelt and put their faces in the dust. Long, solemn blasts from the army's trumpets.

Then Judah turned to the men and gave orders for soldiers to pick up their shields and go after the enemy still holding the citadel. He would need time and safety for the restoration of the sanctuary. Judah turned to the religious men among them, and of those in perfect health, untainted by official, paganized practice, those whose law was love of Torah, from these men he took the priests. And they cleaned the sanctuary, removing the stones on which semen spilled in the official prostitution rites. The altar was also defiled—what should be done with it?

The holy altar could not be destroyed. But it had to be dismantled, the stain of its disgrace was felt too deeply inside them. After hard thinking an idea arose. The altar was pulled down, but the stones were salvaged, stored away in a niche on the Temple Mount, until the day a true prophet, with the authority to make a final decision, would again arise in Israel.

Then they found whole, uncut stones, as written in the Torah, to build a new altar according to the original, ancient plan. They reconstructed the sanctuary and the inner courts, and restored the interior of the Temple. They made new vessels for the religious services, and brought back the Menorah that was saved, the incense holders, the great table. Incense was burned, sweetening the air. The Menorah lamps were lit, and the Temple interior was sanctified with sweet light again. Freshly baked challah shewbread was set on the table, the altar curtains were hung, and new veils were billowing between the prayer courts . . .

On the same day of the year the altar had been desecrated, the Temple devastated by pagans, on

that day three years later singing!—and harps
and lyres and cymbals for the new "hanukkah."
The entire people knelt and put their faces to the
ground, surprised with joy, overcome with the
wealth of a heritage that allowed them this joy.

A hanukkah celebration went on for eight
days, as the people brought peace offerings for
the altar and presents for the Temple. Psalms
were heard as they decorated the altarface with
golden cornices and crowns and small shields.
The gates were restored and the priests' chambers fitted with doors. There was sweet joy as
the shame of desolation was buried by the spirit
of renewal, and a desert of pain bloomed with
the beauty of the people.

The whole congregation of Israel voted to ob-
serve the hanukkah with light in their hearts, at
the same time each year—eight days, beginning
on the twenty-fifth of Kislev.

(4:36–59)

from SECOND BOOK OF
MACCABEES

INTRODUCTION

The Second Book of Maccabees was composed about forty years later than First Maccabees—in approximately 120 B.C.E.—and, unlike First Maccabees, it was probably composed in Greek and based on a much larger work that has been lost. Again I've relied on Kahana's Hebrew version for a sense of the original texture that translation into Western languages obscures. Since Greek was commonly known among Jews of this time, it is certainly no less a Jewish work than First Maccabees—and Second Maccabees displays its bias much more flagrantly than the earlier book.

This bias is an aspect of the popular style of "historical writings" of the time. Since the work is not written in Hebrew, we have less of the biblical echoes of First Maccabees; in place of these echoes, we have highly stylized "visions" and "tales." It is important to recognize the imaginative element in this style and not to read the work too literally.

Second Maccabees confirms much of the historicity of First Maccabees; in fact, it takes a superior attitude to its own authenticity and presumes to correct much of the earlier book. Some of these corrections have stood up, others have been shown to be inflated by partisanship. This partisanship is

colored by Jewish beliefs that were in fashion at the
time in religious circles—for instance, a belief in
physical resurrection after death and an elaborate
justification of martyrdom and sainthood. So we
encounter stories of martyrs and saints in Second
Maccabees that do not appear in First Maccabees.

These tales are embellished for imaginative effect,
but they are clearly grounded in historical events.
We only need to compare the same tales as told in
Third and Fourth Maccabees to see a similar basis in
fact though a wild variation in Greek literary styles.
Third and Fourth Maccabees do not make much pre-
tense at an historical perspective, but seem to be
species of literary sermons, embedded in their time
and place. They are interesting museum pieces.

One important tale found in Second Maccabees
(and retold in different form in Third and Fourth
Maccabees as well as later legends), is the story of
Hannah and her seven sons, all of whom submit to
gruesome tortures and death rather than renounce
their Jewishness. In Second Maccabees, this tale of
martyrdom is told in the most brutal, graphic (and
no doubt accurate) terms, more to emphasize the
preciousness of the life these martyrs were willing
to sacrifice than the attraction of an afterlife. But
vivid ideas of an afterlife were current at the time,
and this tale was embraced first by Jewish sectar-
ians and then by early Christians like Augustine:
the martyrs seemed a type of saint. While this
Christian interpretation helped preserve the book, it
also undermined the literary and Jewish texture of it
by its uncompromisingly literal interpretation. The

passionate stylization of *Second Maccabees* in its imaginative context has often been, at best, misrepresented. I've decided to present a passage that is typical of the style of *Second Maccabees*, the vision of the white horseman, because it contrasts so vividly with an account of the same historical episode in *First Maccabees*.

Second Maccabees doesn't serve the spirit of Hanukkah nearly as well as *First Maccabees*, and it is quite an unrefined work by literary and spiritual standards, but it also contains the most plausible assumptions for the institution of Hanukkah. I've translated these relevant passages, which are too often overlooked in favor of legends of a much later date. The passages about Hanukkah confirm what *First Maccabees* related: Hanukkah was celebrated as a new Sukkot festival.

The celebration of Sukkot, an extremely ancient Jewish festival of independence, is symbolic of a joy not based solely on material victories. Although Judah Maccabee had regained the Temple in Jerusalem, the wars were far from over. But the Maccabees had been brought from despair and the desert back to their home. This return to the Temple is a parallel to the ancient journey in the Sinai desert, where the people lived in booths commemorated in Sukkot ritual—it was in that earlier desert that they survived and eventually were brought to the Torah. So both festivals, Sukkot and Hanukkah, share in a redeeming sense of spiritual awareness based in the real world of battles, disappointments, and deprivation.

from SECOND BOOK OF MACCABEES

A Letter to Jews in Egypt

To our fellow Jews in Egypt: Shalom, from the Jews of Jerusalem and Judea. May God be good to you, in the tradition of the covenant with Abraham, Isaac, and Jacob, who lived to serve him. May you feel the touch of Torah, and its words fill you with grace. May your prayers be heard and bring him closer to you—may you never feel abandoned in times of crisis. Here, we are praying with you in spirit, and for you.

We write to you now as we did during 169 S.B.E. [Seleucid-Babylonian Era—143 B.C.E., the year of Judean independence], when we were persecuted. Then we were desolate, as Jason and his followers turned to the pagans and betrayed us. They burned down the Temple gates and murdered innocent people. But we kept our faith, we were strengthened in prayer, and we overcame.

We returned, reclaiming the Temple: the altar rededicated, the challah shewbread set on the table. The Menorah was lit again. And now we are writing to you, in the year 188 S.B.E. [124

B.C.E.] so you will remember to celebrate the new festival, a new Sukkot for the month of Kislev, as was done at the Hanukkah.

(1:1–10)

The Second Book of Maccabees opens with copies of letters serving as an introduction. The following passage is from a letter of later date than the first, with the same purpose in mind: to remind Jews in exile to celebrate Hanukkah. This passage is followed by a long tale based on the Bible's Book of Nehemiah, in which we learn that when the first Jews returned from Babylonian exile they found some "hidden fire" in the destroyed Temple, which they were later able to use in the first dedication of the Second Temple, during Ezra's time. There is no mention of the later, Talmudic passage about the cruse of oil that was miraculously found in Maccabean times. It seems obvious that the earlier "hanukkah" story in Ezra's day served as an analogue for the Talmudic story.

From Another Letter to Jews in Egypt

We are preparing to celebrate the restoration of the Temple, and we are writing to remind you of the date: the twenty-fifth of Kislev. You may join us by celebrating the days like a Festival of Sukkot.

(1:18)

This passage presents the inauguration of the Hanukkah festival as being of universal, and not just local, Jewish significance.

And so it turned out that the Temple restoration was made on the same day—the twenty-fifth of the same month, Kislev—which was remembered as the day of its pagan desecration, three years before. The celebration went on for eight happy days, like the Festival of Sukkot, in the awareness that not many days earlier they were observing the Sukkot festival while hiding out in caves and wandering like wild animals in the mountains.

That is the reason they carried branches of fruit trees and palm-fronds, and they sang psalms to the Lord: it was their faith that brought them back to his Temple.

In an unusual innovation, they passed a law for the festival, affecting the entire nation of Jews around the world. They voted that all Jews, not only those in Jerusalem, should share in this happy festival each year.

(10:5–8)

This passage occurs in the same place in the narrative of Maccabean battles as the prayer of Judah in First Maccabees. Judah and his men prepare for the successful battle with Greek forces (which, in addition to outnumbering Judah's, contain many Jewish apostates). The victory

*enables the Jewish forces to enter Jerusalem, rededicate
the Temple, and celebrate the first Hanukkah festival.
But here, instead of quoting a prayer, the composer of
Second Maccabees supplies a stylized visionary episode
to serve the same emotional purpose that the composer of
First Maccabees supplied in the prayer. Most of the tales
in Second Maccabees, while fabricated with great zeal,
are not as disarming as this one.*

About eighty thousand foot soldiers, many
more thousands of cavalry, and eighty elephants
armored for war were massed against the Jews.
Jerusalem was to become once and for all a city
of Greeks . . .

Lysias entered Judea at Beth Zur, an important fortified city twenty miles from Jerusalem,
and it was immediately surrounded. As soon as
Maccabee and his men heard of this, they
spread the news among the Jews, who were
heartsick. And with tears in their eyes, they
prayed to the Lord, and they hoped in their
hearts a good angel would be with Israel.

But they took their fate in their own hands—
Judah himself was the first to prepare his
weapons, and he was an example to the rest for
courage in the face of ugly odds. They were
going to risk their lives to save their brothers at
the front line. With the resolve of a single man
rising to his feet, the entire group prepared for
battle.

They had only just left Jerusalem when suddenly, at the head of their column, leading them

forward, was a horseman dressed in white, weapons and armor flashing of gold. Then, as if all the men together had but one voice, a shout went up to the Lord who had showed them a vision of mercy.

And they were filled with a strength of spirit, making them fearless before men, ready to take on even the most savage animal, ready to break through walls of iron. They marched into battle as if heaven was their ally, as if an angel were leading them. They charged the enemy, they hurled themselves like lions against them . . .

(11:1–11)

from THE BOOK OF DANIEL

INTRODUCTION

Some chapters of the Bible's Book of Daniel are written in Jewish Aramaic, the lingua franca in Judea during the time of its composition in the second century B.C.E. The following portion is from the eleventh chapter, which is composed in Hebrew. It is on this chapter that modern scholars have based their dating of the composition between 167 and 164 B.C.E. This places the book in genuine Maccabean times—actually just before the success of the Maccabean revolt and during the Greek persecution under King Antiochus Epiphanes. As with all the biblical books, the date of composition does not refer to the date of the original materials: much of Daniel existed in fragment and legend actually dating back to the Babylonian exile.

Chapter eleven describes the wars within the Greek empire in great detail. It is unlike any other biblical prophecy in its manner, though its description of events that are already history is traditional. It is composed in prophetic form (while aware that the age of prophecy has passed) for many reasons; one important consideration was to transcend the political arena, and while the Hellenized Jew would view the chapter as an obscurely mystical work, the understanding Jew would see it as an inspirational

*one. And it seems to have achieved popularity
among these Jews as a work supporting the Maccabean revolt and the resistance to Greek paganism.*

*While Daniel was composed well before the
Books of Maccabees, it supports a similar sense of
triumphant martyrdom. But unlike them, it is
firmly based in a biblical context and is rich with
biblical echoes and parallelisms. It appears especially close to the imagery developed in the prophet
Ezekiel, but also resembles other books near the
Maccabean era in its historical perspective dating
back to the first fall of Jerusalem in 606 B.C.E. In this
context as well, the figure of Daniel is a later version of the Suffering Servant image in Isaiah, a kind
of transition point from the older prophetic sense of
the communal remnant of survivors to the later
rabbinic sense of individual saintliness—both being
responses to the similar tragedy of Jewish suffering.*

*But Daniel is especially important for an under-
standing of Hanukkah not because of its consolation
to the persecuted Jews, but because it provides the
context in which to understand both the depth of
passion in the Maccabean resistance and the long
historical tradition from which the Maccabean
Hanukkah arises. This latest of Jewish festivals has
survived not because of its secular or religious func-
tion. It's the only post-biblical festival that is fixed
in the Jewish calendar because it is deeply rooted in
Jewish history. Beyond its ancient root in Sukkot, it
contains and transforms the memory of the first loss
of Jerusalem, the Babylonian exile, and the return*

to Jerusalem. In this sense, it can also project for-
ward and through Jewish history to our day—the
Roman destruction, the long exile and diaspora, and
the modern return to Israel.

from THE BOOK OF DANIEL

*Chapter eleven of Daniel begins by telescoping a few
hundred years of history into a few stanzas, starting with
King Xerxes of Persia during the time of the Babylonian
exile up to King Alexander of Greece. This is a popular
form of history, with the dramatic literary convention of
having it come from the mouth of an angel—no one at
the time, approximately 165 B.C.E., was likely to believe
that angels were prophesying history in Babylon. Of
course, there's a "suspension of disbelief" on the reader's
or hearer's part, just as there would be in ancient Greek
drama when gods and half-gods were speaking: the audience identifies with deep emotional truths in Daniel, not
"literal" truths. (Not that the historical survey isn't accurate, especially in the details almost contemporary
with the Maccabean Age.) Deeper yet, spiritual revelations are possible because the historical and cultural context supports a communal tradition—in Israel's case, already a thousand years at the time of this chapter of
Daniel.*

*This first passage runs to the death of Alexander the
Great, who was considered a great friend of the Jews, and
then describes the breakup of his kingdom after his death.*

And now I will tell you
the truth as it unfolds
beyond the present page—

before the ink can flow from the pen
look: three more kings
succeed each other in Persia

and then a fourth, the richest yet
translating wealth to power
itching to challenge Greece

but there, in Greece, the strongest king
the world has ever seen
arises, doing as he pleases

and as he perches on his world empire
he dies, his kingdom falls
cracks apart

into four pieces like the four winds:
north, south, east, and west
none into the hands of his descendants

and none of his successors can put together
the strength that was his
for it is torn up by the roots

transplanted to yet more petty dynasties
by yet others than these
and mercilessly cultivated . . .

(11:2–4)

This passage describes the advent of Antiochus Epiphanes, who claims the throne of the Asian part of the Greek empire, the Seleucid kingdom. The "prince over people of the covenant" refers to the Jewish province of the Greek empire in Judea.

And then standing in his place
is the unrecognized—ignored
as if he'd been a harmless dolt

who then, when least suspected
scheming behind the scenes
seizes control

all opposition will be swept away
like water jars in a flood
and smashed—even the prince

over people of the covenant
is lost—
and even though his loyal party is small

anyone making peace with him
is drawn into a maelstrom
by a treacherous hand;

in placid, peaceful times
he will storm into the richest provinces
and succeed and be accepted

as if in a dream
all his detractors suddenly paralyzed
a fact his fathers wouldn't dare to dream

so unscrupulous the royal hand
that grabs like a thief
to reward just the loyal bullies

and with all this even he will dream
of conquering more fortress cities
and he will—but only for a while . . .

(11:21–24)

King Antiochus Epiphanes has consolidated his rule and has just fought a successful battle against a Ptolemy, the Egyptian representative of the Greek empire. Then he will again invade Egypt ("the South"), but this time he is turned back and vents his frustration on the Jews. Many of the Jews have become paganized according to his decrees, but others are strengthened in their resistance by the king's self-identification with the highest god of the world. (Coins of this time show Antiochus Epiphanes in the likeness of a Greek god.) This portion of Daniel offers comfort to the persecuted Jews by setting this king in an historical and political perspective that reduces him to mortal size. But he remains an archetypal figure, whether projected back into history as the Nebuchadnezzar in the Book of Judith, or projected forward into our own century as a German or Russian dictator.

Then this king of the north
will turn back for home
followed by a long train of riches

now his mind has turned
to the people of the covenant
his heart set against its Temple

he will set his hand against it
as he passes through the land
before returning home

in a while he'll set out again
invading the south
but now the scene has changed

and in the background ships from Kittim: the
        west
Roman ships
he will be cowed and turn around

and with his mind sunk in rage
he will growl at the people
of the covenant, ravaging the Temple

rewarding the cowards who turn
against their own religion
then he will unleash his forces

to enter the Temple inner sanctuary
desecrate it
demolish the gates

beat and demean the pious there
defile the altar
set up idols

that make one fall to his knees
not in submission, not in humility
but in utter desolation

those who are eager to submit to power
to lick the feet of foreigners
will be soothed and flattered—for a time

they will slander their own heritage
but those who know a God in their hearts
have an inner strength to resist

and they are beacons of conscience
in the midst of flames
some will be burnt at the stake

or pierced or crucified
or thrown into slavery
tortured, maimed, robbed

but they will continue teaching
and be helped by some who are fighting
even those fighting blindly only for themselves

and those who resist with the openness in their
        hearts
even as they fall their teaching shines
like metal in the fire: refined

and purified and a healing
for the people to rise and continue
even as no end is yet in sight

the king appears to grow stronger
as if magnified in a mirror
free to strut in his own image

flattering himself above the gods
so arrogantly inflated
he sees himself as the highest god

speaking out of such swollen pride
as if his heart was engraved on iron
to last forever

and it will seem so until the wrath
like his life
is exhausted.

                        (11:28–36)

A BLAZING FOUNTAIN

Zechariah
from the **Torah**
Kings
Ezra
from the **Hallel**

INTRODUCTION

In this section the works are drawn from the Hebrew Bible (Tanakh, or Old Testament) and unlike
the Book of Daniel (also from the Bible) considera-
bly predate the Maccabean Age. Their connection
with Hanukkah observance was established with
the calendar of Torah reading in synagogues, before
the medieval legends. And these works are part of
the observance today. The reading and study of the
Bible in synagogues (making it available to the mass
of people) actually began in Maccabean times and is
intimately bound up with the Maccabean spirit of
confrontation.

The title work, "A Blazing Fountain," is the special haftorah portion for the shabbat of Hanukkah;
and since it is also used at another shabbat during
the liturgical year, many young boys and girls have
learned to chant this passage in Hebrew for their
bar or bat mitzvah.

"A Blazing Fountain," like the menorah itself, is
central to an understanding of Hanukkah's power.
This portion from the prophet Zechariah, composed
three hundred years before the Maccabean revolt,
with its climactic stanza a famous touchstone for
Judaism as well as all monotheistic religions ("not
by force, not by power, but by my spirit, says the

Lord"), *especially needs a creative interpretation. As a prefiguration of both a renewed Jewish state and the spiritual force of the Hanukkah festival, it provided a foundation in the Bible unparalleled in beauty. Hanukkah is known both as the Festival of Dedication (of the Temple) and the Festival of Lights, and "A Blazing Fountain" attempts to fuse the two in modern imagery that grows out of the original Hebrew.*

The unusual imagery of a fountain ablaze with light is typical of the prophet's vision of spiritual and political renewal. Far from describing a national or religious victory, it faces up to the spiritual failures of the past and the inadequacies of material power. It is a witness to the first return from Babylonian captivity in 537 B.C.E., less than fifty years after the destruction of Jerusalem, and the hanukkah (dedication) of the altar for the second Temple. Historically speaking, this would be the third hanukkah—the first taking place for the ark in Sinai, and the second for Solomon's dedication of the first Temple.

In one sense, Hanukkah commemorates the birth of the Jewish "religion," as distinct from the Jewish nation—an institution above and beyond and supporting the physical state and ethnic nation. In this portion of Zechariah, the coming together of state (symbolized by Zerubbavel) and religion (symbolized by Joshua) is not a wedding but a revelation of the spiritual dimension to all worldly renewals. And so it is a further elaboration of the first "hanukkah," when Moses built the ark in Sinai, more than a thousand years before the Maccabean Hanukkah.

The portion read from the Torah during Hanukkah describes the dedication of the altar and completion of the ark in the desert, approximately 1225 B.C.E. I've translated the passage describing the making of the first Menorah. There is an intimation of the Maccabean Hanukkah attached to this passage in the midrash of Nachmanides, who interprets Aaron's understanding that this first dedication will have a deeper fulfillment many centuries later.

When there is a second shabbat that falls within the eight days of Hanukkah, there is another special haftorah for Hanukkah. The passage from the First Book of Kings describes the building of the first Temple and preparations for its dedication—the second hanukkah, approximately 950 B.C.E. The portion I've translated is a brief inventory following the preceding, wonderfully detailed description— it's as if the author was so immersed in his description that he had to stop and go over it again in order to contain a sense of the whole work in one thought. Earlier, all of these items were more intricately described: their sizes, the designs of lions, oxen, cherubim, palm trees, chariot, the great Sea, and the details of the ornamental work on everything.

Following this inventory passage, the Temple will be dedicated as the ark is brought up to Jerusalem from Shiloh, containing nothing but the two stone tablets that Moses put there during the

*first hanukkah. And then comes the sublime de-
scription of the Lord's spirit descending into the
Room of the Word, or Holy of Holies—described in
terms resonant of the Lord's earlier presence in
Sinai.*

*The vessels of the Sanctuary described in this in-
ventory are ostensibly the same vessels that will be
looted by the Babylonians, returned by favor of the
Persians, and then looted again by the Greeks from
the second Temple, during Maccabean times, almost eight hundred years later.*

*The Book of Ezra was probably composed in the
fourth century* B.C.E., *and contains many older
fragments contemporary with the prophet Zechariah and the actual Ezra, following the return from
Babylonian exile. Passages from Ezra have often
been read during Hanukkah because of their description of events leading to this earlier hanukkah
of the second Temple.*

*The passage I've interpreted portrays the scene
following the dedication of the new altar. The Temple has not yet been rebuilt, but the work has be-
gun. It has been perhaps fifty years since the first
Temple was destroyed. The people's response to this
earlier hanukkah prefigures the Maccabean spirit of
the Hanukkah festival. Joy, but not untempered by
realism (Jerusalem was a shadow of its former self);
and an intuition of the difficulties ahead.*

*The emotions of joy and relief at survival are
given their widest scope in the series of psalms*

known as the Hallel (Psalms 113 through 118),
chanted by the singers and musicians of the Temple.
The Talmud pays the deepest respect to the historicity and importance of the Hanukkah festival simply by confirming that the Hallel was to be recited
for the full eight days, as it is during the biblical
Sukkot festival.

I have translated Psalm 114 from the Hallel,
evoking the emotional response to the earlier gain-
ing of liberty from the Egyptians. It was also felt as
miraculous, supremely so, and deepens the historical perspective all the way back to before the time
the Torah was received at Mount Sinai. The miracles of the desert evoked in this psalm are clearly
poeticized, communicating the spirit in which sur-
prising reversals appear miraculous in their historical context. And the events they relate to—crossing
the Red Sea, and the later parallels of crossing the
Jordan into Israel and finally the Kingdom of Israel
(or Judah) itself—refer to the communal history in a
heady, more personalized way than the Torah. I've
tried to clarify the individual perspective of the
poet, in his animation of historical events, by
sharpening the focus of personal surprise and exultation, especially implied in the way the psalm
ends.

Josephus, the Jewish Roman historian, described
the Maccabean Hanukkah festival as a celebration
of a "miracle": the miracle of achieving "liberty
beyond our hopes." The spirit of that achievement
is mirrored in the Hallel, psalms of praise and
thanksgiving.

A BLAZING FOUNTAIN

The Hanukkah Haftorah
from the Prophet Zechariah

Sing like a skylark
happy being home
daughter of Zion

because I am coming
to join you
with the sky you hoped for

over you
sky of your deepest dream
infinite sky

of reality
you dared to see
in the midst of a fogbound world

I will be in the midst of you
as true as your eyes
see through a clear blue sky

and I will be inside of you
as you were open to me   light
in a world suppressed in darkness

leadenly earthbound
giants in their mirror
hearing only themselves

and the gargoyles of their unconscious
but light is the voice of your creator
breaking through you

in the midst of the world
and many nations will see it
dawn breaking on that day

all will join me in the light
of reality   warm
beneath an infinite wing

and you will know my breath is sent
the man who is speaking to you
by the Lord our creator

who will breathe in Israel
once again enfolding his daughter
Zion in the holy land

holding Jerusalem
· small reflection
in the pupil of an eye

beholding him again
beneath an azure sky
calm inside

be quiet be still
all people of flesh
before the Lord

a sky of promise is unfolding
before us
the horizon expands

to include earth and sky
and the small voice within
will break out singing.

Then the Lord allowed me to see
in a vision
the high priest Joshua

in a court in heaven
the judge the Lord's angel
(the word for divine agent)

to his right the satan
(the word for accuser)
accusing him

and the word of the Lord
said to the satan
May the Lord reject your words hard accuser

the Lord who chooses Jerusalem
rejects your flood of venom
this man is but an ashen stick

plucked from the fire—
Joshua's clothes were filthy
as he stood before the angel—

who was saying to those in the heavenly court
take off his poor and filthy clothes
and turning to him was saying: look

I have removed your guilt
and dress you in clean robes—
and then it was I who was saying:

let them put a clean turban on his head!
and they did
and he was splendidly dressed

as the Lord's angel watched
then to Joshua slowly said
(matching the depth of his attention)

these are the words of the Lord
if you will walk through your life
in my ways

and keep my presence there
in the people's life
you will be head of my house

and present in my court
free to come and go
in this heavenly court

listen Joshua   high priest
you and your new pioneers
are signs of the growth coming

you are like new shoots
and I will bring you
a new branch a new line

the man growing from my promise
as from a root
in the promised land

look at this stone it has eyes
I reveal to Joshua
seven facets seven eyes

cornerstone of a new day
on which I engrave
the living inscription the promise

that on that one day —
I will remove
the dirty clothes and guilt

from the shoulders of this land
and in your lightness
you will see every man your neighbor

and call to him
(the words of the Lord are speaking)
come sit on this good earth with me

beneath my fig tree
(each will be truly at home)
and my ripening vine.

Then the angel returned
startling me with words
as if life was a dreamy silent movie

until an angel spoke to me
saying what do you see
and my words like an unblinking camera

showed me a golden menorah
a golden bowl above it
brimming with oil

fed from two olive trees
standing on each side
there are seven lights

fed by the golden oil
so that it's always lit
by the trees

seven golden flames
lit by trees
like a blazing fountain

then I turned to the angel
speaking again
in words of conversation

what are these things my Lord
I've described
through the camera of vision

you don't know how to read then
what you've written?
spoke the angel that was there

conversing with me
and I was saying
no my Lord

then he answered
and was saying
these words

this is the word of the Lord
(immediate vision)
to Zerubbavel the governor

not by force
not by power
but by my spirit

says the Lord
what are you
worldly mountain

of all material things
and earthbound forces
compared to Zerubbavel?

you are nothing a false shrine
leveled to the ground
and he will hold up the crowning headstone

that was highest once beneath the sky
and it will be a cornerstone
of azure

and all will step back deeply in awe
of pure beauty
singing the grace of spirit.

(2:14–4:7)

NUMBERS (BEMIDBAR)

From the Torah Portion Read during Hanukkah

The Lord spoke to Moshe
in these words
saying

you will speak to Aaron
and these will be your words:
As you prepare the seven lights

set them in the Menorah
so that each throws its light equally forward
seven lights separate, but one illumination

and this is how Aaron did it
the lights blazing distinct, but as one
from the holy Menorah

each of the lights shining equally forward
just as the Lord commanded
in the words Moshe heard

And here is the Menorah:
the base, the branches and flowers
all of it a single piece

beaten out of gold
a solid plate of gold
hammered into the pattern shown to Moshe

by the Lord—
this pattern was followed by the artist
in making the Menorah.

(8:1–4)

THE FIRST BOOK OF KINGS

From the Haftorah Portion Read during the Second Shabbat of Hanukkah

So the artist Hiram also made the pots
the shovels and the bowls
and with these had finished the work
in the Lord's Temple
as commissioned by King Solomon:
the two pillars and their lily-work
and on top of the pillars, the capitals
molded like bowls and shaped like lilies
and to complete these a set of filigree
    chain-work for each
and the four hundred pomegranates for the two
    sets of filigree
two rows of pomegranates for each
winding around the capitals on the pillars
and the ten stands
ten basins on each stand
and the one Sea
twelve brass oxen beneath it for support
and the pots, the shovels, the bowls—
all of these furnishings, even the vessels
made of burnished brass by Hiram
for the Lord's Temple

and Solomon had them sandcast in the plain of
    Jordan
between Succot and Tzaretan
huge molds made from clay in the Jordan valley
and so many vessels were made
so much brass used in the furnishings
that the weighing of them all was never
    organized
so this we cannot know—
but all the furnishings to be used
in the house of the Lord
were made only by Solomon—
also the special altar for incense
inlaid with gold
and the table made of gold for the shewbread
    loaves
and the menorahs of red gold
five on each side of the Sanctuary
and the lights for them, the flowers, the tongs
all of gold
and the cups and the snuffers
the firepans, sprinkling bowls, censers
of red gold
and the hinges for the doors
of the inner house: the Room of the Word
were made of gold
as were the hinges for the outer doors
to the Sanctuary and Temple—

So when all the works for the Temple
were finished by King Solomon

only then he brought in the sacred things
consecrated by his father, David
the silver, the gold, the vessels
all this treasure was put away
in the storerooms
of the Lord's Temple.

(7:40 –51)

THE BOOK OF EZRA

The workers had built up the foundation
of the Lord's Temple
the original outline was visible again

Cohens (priests) were there in their robes
they blew the trumpets of assembly
Levis were there with cymbals and lyres

as Asaph had been directed
by David, King of Israel
in his day

and they sang back and forth to each other
antiphonally
"Sing praises to the Lord in psalms

so good it is to be singing"
and the refrain:
"His mercy sings through us

to Israel
as it has
and always will"

Then all the people broke out in song
because the house of the Lord
was rising again

but many of the oldest Cohens and Levis
and heads of families
old men who had seen the first house

and who could see it still standing
fixed in their memories—
these men broke out weeping

loudly, openly
as they stood before this house
rising again in their living eyes

many others were shouting joyfully
a great noise was going up
people in the distance could hear it clearly

and they could not tell by their ears
the sound of weeping
from the sound of joy.

(3:10–13)

from the HALLEL

Psalm 114

When Israel came out of Egypt
like a child suddenly free
from a people of strange speech

Judah became a home
for the Children of Israel
as they became a Sanctuary

for the God of their fathers—
the House of Israel
were brought into the open

and as the Sea saw them coming
it ran from the sight
the Jordan stopped dead in its tracks

mountains leaped like frightened rams
hills were a scattering flock
of lambs

What was so alarming, Sea?
Jordan, what vision
drained your strength away?

Mountains, why did you quake
like fearful rams?
Hills, why did you jump like lambs?

All Earth, tremble
in the presence
of your maker

it was the God of Jacob
and he is here
all around you

a sudden pool of water
from a desert rock
a fountain from wilderness stone—

life from a heart of stone
and from bitter tears
a sweet land.

ILLUMINATIONS

Lighting the Menorah

The Little Prayer for First Night
Only (Shehecheyanu)

These Singing Lights
(Hanerot Hallalu)

Rock of All My Dreams
(Maoz Tzur)

We Remember the Miraculous
(Al Hanissim)

from the Talmud (Shabbat 21b)

Psalm for Making Hanukkah
(Psalm 30)

Psalm from a "Great Hallel"
(Psalm 121)

INTRODUCTION

Hanukkah did not have a secular emphasis like many other Jewish holidays now long forgotten. There was a "Feast of Lights," but no "Feast of Maccabees." Just as "A Blazing Fountain" described how Hanukkah was anchored to ancient tradition via images of the Menorah, when we come to post-Maccabean prayers and commentary the menorah is central.

According to the Talmud, a menorah (which simply means "lampstand") is not to be made as a replica of the seven-branched original in the Temple. The first Hanukkah menorahs looked nothing like the Temple version that became the popular emblem for Israel; instead, they resembled the oriental lamps in common use. The eight- or nine-branched imitations of the Temple Menorah now accepted were not seen until the Middle Ages in Europe. And so the form of a Hanukkah menorah is open to creative interpretation, within certain limitations designed to keep it from resembling the pagan types or suggesting the Greek winter festival during which bonfires were held sacred to pagan gods—each flame of the menorah burns distinctively, and should not be allowed to merge with the next.

The prayers for "Lighting the Menorah" follow traditional formulae, commonly translated into English beginning "Blessed art Thou, O Lord our God, King of the Universe . . ." This English formula has lost most of the living resonance it once had. Even in the original Hebrew, the image of a "King of the Universe" had greater immediacy in a time when kingship was the way of the world. In its original context, then, to recognize such a universal "king" is to ridicule worldly pretensions of exclusive power. It is a deeply antimaterialistic image, this melech ha-olam, and it's necessary to revitalize the imagery in translation, to personalize it. This is less of an issue in Hebrew, and the prayers should be recited in the original language, carrying both an ancient and modern resonance.

These little prayers are as alternately tender and iconoclastic as any ancient Greek lyric ever was. In the mouth of a humble individual, these blessings simultaneously demolish and transcend the material sanctity invested in worldly power.

As well as commemorating a victory over idolatry, the Hanukkah literature also preserves the same spirit of Jewish resistance to idolatrous practice as do the prophets. When Jewish practice adopted pagan forms, whether lampstands or prayers, the process of transformation to a Jewish context also meant a demystification of pagan ritualization—in short, a devastating irony directed against mystery religions as well as worldly power. The "miracles" of Hanukkah, whether the recovery of Jerusalem or the recovery of a cruse of undefiled oil for the Temple Menorah, became gentle parables for a sense of historical realism: the renewals that a faith based in the universe of time allows.

"These Singing Lights" is typical of this attitude to miracles—man-made, but based in a spiritual awareness. The lights of Hanukkah are as gentle as this prayer itself, and as firm as its joy in the process of renewal. The deep image of this prayer superimposes the ancient spirit of the Hallel psalms onto the lights themselves: the lights hallalu *is how it begins. This prayer more than any other shows how boldly the Jews resisted the Greek rites for the Rural Dionysia. During Maccabean times large numbers of secularized Jews observed the holiday of the dominant Greek culture—the pagan fires and torches were as prevalent as Christmas trees in North America. It took a large spirit to* transform *that practice.*

"Rock of All My Dreams" is an adaptation of the first stanza and refrain of Maoz Tzur, a medieval Hebrew poem freely translated into English as the Christian hymn, "Rock of Ages." Translations of Maoz Tzur are usually free adaptations of the Hebrew, since the original is composed in a complicated rhyme, meter, and acrostic form, coming out as highly stylized language. The poem was later sung to a medieval German hymn, and this tune survives today and is intimately bound up with the words.

Any English translation attempting to fit the same music will probably sound stilted, if not downright ridiculous. And the slavish adherence to the medieval European rhyme and meter and music is quite out of step with the serious character of the poem. The Hebrew poem, like ancient Hebrew psalms, was not written to fit a melody like pop songs. Today we chant the psalms of the Hallel in a form that perhaps derives from days of the Temple in Jerusalem, but even then the chanting is projected onto the composition, rather than determining its form.

So I wanted to suggest in English a sense of the immediacy to the original poem, to make a modern adaptation with a sense of spokenness. I wanted it not to sound like a museumpiece when you say it aloud and not to look like a singsong when you read it. I've made a version for reading, after the singing of the original Hebrew, but I've limited myself to the first and most well-known stanza. The later verses of Maoz Tzur go on to describe the crises of historical "pasts" and the ensuing "rededications" of Jewish history, on up to the Hanukkah festival of rededication: the ancient Egyptian persecution, the Babylonian destruction, the Persian threat of annihilation, and finally the Greek reign of oppression. So Maoz Tzur also serves to anchor Hanukkah in the long Jewish tradition that is more authentically felt in "A Blazing Fountain."

The ancient prayer of "We Remember the Miraculous" (Al Hanissim) predates the Talmud's explanation of Hanukkah, and in it the process of Judaism's transformation into a major world religion is visible. Al Hanissim was written perhaps in the first century C.E., before the Roman destruction of the Temple, and the Talmud's parable of the miraculous cruse of oil is not yet envisioned. But Hanukkah was already an established festival and needed an historical explanation. Here the miracle of Hanukkah is the recovery of the Temple in Jerusalem and with it the whole complex of religious, ethical, and historical traditions going back to Sinai.

At the time of this prayer the Temple and tradition are still intact. Later, the Talmud will find the Temple's Menorah symbolic of this recovery (eight hundred years after Solomon built the first Temple). Because it will turn out that this "hanukkah," or dedication of the Temple, is the last one, the whole tradition will undergo a deeper transformation, beginning with the Talmud, bringing us to the Judaism we know today. Hanukkah will remain as the last festival to be recognized as an integral link in the tradition.

As it happens, the Hanukkah menorah becomes the miracle itself: just as Hanukkah commemorates the saving of Judaism and the need to renew its original power, the home menorah commemorates the further miracle of its survival beyond the Temple, so that the lights are symbolic of the imaginative

*resources needed to renew the tradition. A later
rabbinic tradition interprets the Talmud's parable of
the single surviving cruse of oil as a metaphor for
Mattathias himself, since his was one home in
which the light of Judaism remained pure, and from
it the original spirit was rekindled. The Talmud's
story, then, is a domestication of the Temple tradition, just as Hanukkah was to become a domestic
holiday.*

*In this prayer the original Hanukkah menorah
lights are lit in the Temple courtyards, and the actual Temple menorah is not mentioned. Here the
eight days of the Hanukkah festival are still a reflection of its root in the eight days of Sukkot, the major
festival of light and rejoicing prescribed in the Torah. Sukkot was the major light and Hanukkah its
true reflection. But just as the Talmud's menorah
parable has another level as an historical link to the
oil from the first Temple (found by Ezra and used to
rededicate the altar after the Babylonian exile), the
Hanukkah menorah and its lighting is the only
physical memorial of a Temple service that survives
today.*

*The portion from the Talmud that refers to
Hanukkah is highly refined into a few short passages, developed perhaps three or four centuries
after the Maccabeans. Immediately preceding the
central passage which I've translated—and which
is the source for later, more diffuse legends—is an
account of a conflict between two opposing view-*

points on the lighting of menorah lights. The view-
point that lost out held that eight lights should be lit
on the first day, diminishing in number until the last
day of Hanukkah when only one light remains—
from this point of view, the ultimate loss of the
Temple is central and is thus commemorated, each
day of diminishing light returning us to the di-
minished reality we now must live in. The School of
Hillel, which prevailed, seems to set Hanukkah in a
larger perspective, linking the menorah tradition
backwards through the Temple and forwards
through the confidence in further miraculous renewals. The importance of the Hanukkah festival
today, in Israel as in North America, appears to
bear out this early insight in the Talmud.

In the context of the Talmud itself, Hanukkah on
the whole does not receive the attention that other
festivals do: as the last festival to be recognized, its
spiritual power was still embryonic, though intui-
tively recognized, and this is reflected in the power
of parable contained in the passage I've presented.
It is very difficult to isolate a passage from the Talmud because its world of discourse is so resonant.
Yet just a fairly literal translation, while losing almost everything of the original flavor, at least
shows, in its stark simplicity, how moving a direct
contact with authentic sources is, and usually pref-
erable to later, secondary retellings. Later "stories
of Hanukkah," whether represented as sanitized
fairy tale, military adventure, or sentimental
dogma, often alienate children as well as adults, re-

sulting in a diminution of the festival's spirit. What is untranslatable, though, in a small section from the Talmud, is a sense of its process at work. The Talmud is fundamentally self-critical in its approach, and simplistic solutions to the reasons for things are anathema to it. It addresses itself equally to prosaic reality and the deepest mystery of the Torah, and what is a "miracle" can be a very down-to-earth way of looking at things.

Beyond this passage about Hanukkah, it should be noted that the Talmud itself responded to the same pressures as the Maccabean revolt. Guided by the Pharisees, public study of the Torah, especially the reading and interpretation of it in synagogues, dates from Maccabean times—in reaction to Hellenism. The Pharisees, in opposition to the priestly and ruling classes, also developed subtle powers of exegesis in binding the written Torah to the oral one, and the Talmud developed along the same lines. But the Pharisaic emphasis on democratizing religion and popularizing the Bible grew out of a need to strengthen Judaism, and it is the same need which leads to popularization of the Hanukkah festival. So Hanukkah, like all Jewish festivals, should direct a person back to its original sources.

"Psalm for Making Hanukkah" (Psalm 30) is subtitled in the Bible "A Psalm of Hanukkah" because it was probably used at the "hanukkah" of the second Temple in Ezra's time. But it is the one psalm traditionally connected to the Hanukkah festival, and I've used the phrase "high praises" in translation to echo the Hallel. It is understood that the personal and the collective are interchangeable in this, as in most psalms. I have emphasized its personal context, which is also the traditional interpretation, ascribing its composition to King David. If it were actually written by David, it would have been composed in the tenth century B.C.E. and predate the first Temple. Whether or not this is true, the psalm adds another layer to the historic foundation of the Hanukkah festival. And the resonance is broadened in the autobiographical sense of correspondence to David's life, who brought Israel to Jerusalem. There was more than one occasion in David's life when he could have composed this psalm, combining a sense of spiritual wonder with the fallibility of the human ego, and a passionate affirmation of the inseparability of religious and secular identity.

"The Songs of Ascent," the psalms beginning with Psalm 120, are traditionally thought of as a "Great Hallel." They were perhaps chanted by the Levis as they ascended steps within the Temple. They were also favored by Jews on pilgrimage to Jerusalem—something every Jew hoped to do at least once in his or her lifetime—since one ascends the surrounding hills and mountains to reach the city. And the central "mountain" in Jerusalem would be Mount Zion, on which the Temple stood.

"Psalm from a 'Great Hallel' "(Psalm 121) has often been considered especially appropriate for

Hanukkah, with its exultation in wonder of liberty and perpetual renewal. It is also an affirmation of victory over material pride and of faith in Israel's nationhood, set in a universal context.

A reading of these two personal psalms, 30 and 121, with their roots in the ancient Temple, is an appropriate way to match the menorah's illumination of Hanukkah in the home.

ILLUMINATIONS

The Home Service

This section contains the home service for the nights of Hanukkah. Since it takes only a few minutes, each home finds other free-spirited activities (as dreidel playing has served since medieval times) to honor the injunction for the menorah lights that says: no work for thirty minutes after lighting, in order to appreciate their flames.

One candle is lit for each night of the festival, in addition to the "servant" candle which is always lit first and then used to light the actual Hanukkah candles. On the first night only, in addition to the two kindling prayers, the Shehecheyanu is said—but on all nights these prayers are said before lighting the lights. (It is more or less customary to light the servant candle before saying these prayers, holding it in hand while reciting them.)

The lights are placed in the menorah from right to left, starting with one for the first night, then two on the second, until all eight are lit on the last night. But the candles are actually to be lit from left to right, so that the additional light of each night is kindled first.

After the first light is kindled by the servant light, stop and recite Hanerot Hallalu ("These Singing Lights"), and then kindle the remaining lights.

The lights should burn at least half an hour and, especially for those living on the first floor, the menorah should be set in the window, so that people still coming home from work will be reminded what day it is. Traditionally, the lights are lit upon appearance of the stars, but it is okay to light them at any time of the night, as long as others in the home are still awake.

   Immediately after the lights are lit, Maoz Tzur ("Rock of All My Dreams") is sung or recited.

LIGHTING THE MENORAH

First Prayer

You are deeply felt
Lord beyond lords

the ends of the universe
are just a crown for you

a gem from your throne
is the rock in our hearts

you gave us the grace
to learn your desire

and in the presence of your desire
we light the flame of Hanukkah.

הדלקת נרות חנוכה

בָּרוּךְ אַתָּה

יְיָ אֱלֹהֵינוּ

מֶלֶךְ הָעוֹלָם

אֲשֶׁר קִדְּשָׁנוּ בְּמִצְוֹתָיו

וְצִוָּנוּ לְהַדְלִיק נֵר שֶׁל חֲנֻכָּה.

LIGHTING THE MENORAH

Second Prayer

You are deeply felt
Lord beyond lords

the ends of the universe
are just a crown for you

a gem from your throne
is the rock in our hearts

you made your presence miraculously alive
in the eyes of our mothers and fathers

in ancient days
yet in these very days of the year.

בָּרוּךְ אַתָּה

יְיָ אֱלֹהֵינוּ

מֶלֶךְ הָעוֹלָם

שֶׁעָשָׂה נִסִּים לַאֲבוֹתֵינוּ

בַּיָּמִים הָהֵם בַּזְּמַן הַזֶּה.

LIGHTING THE MENORAH

The Little Prayer for First Night Only
(Shehecheyanu)

You are deeply felt
Lord beyond lords

the ends of the universe
are just a crown for you

a gem from your throne
is the rock in our hearts

you kept our body alive
you kept our spirit alive

you allowed us to arrive
at these days of the year.

בָּרוּךְ אַתָּה
יְיָ אֱלֹהֵינוּ
מֶלֶךְ הָעוֹלָם
שֶׁהֶחֱיָנוּ וְקִיְּמָנוּ
וְהִגִּיעָנוּ לַזְּמַן הַזֶּה.

THESE SINGING LIGHTS

Hanerot Hallalu

These singing lights
we light to remember
the miracle of our survival
the miraculous victories and deliverances
out of wars and ashes
that sang in the eyes of our mothers and fathers
at these very days of the year
just as the priests used to sing in the Temple
in ancient days

Through the full eight days of Hanukkah
these singing lights are deeply felt
for their light is not to see by
not to use in the ordinary world
but to behold and feel
like a memory deep within—
like a chord of praise
struck by light
inspiring us to sing
in the name of what's held holy
that we have been delivered to this day
in the miracle of our lives.

הַנֵּרוֹת הַלָּלוּ
אֲנַחְנוּ מַדְלִיקִין
עַל הַנִּסִּים
וְעַל הַנִּפְלָאוֹת וְעַל הַתְּשׁוּעוֹת
וְעַל הַמִּלְחָמוֹת
שֶׁעָשִׂיתָ לַאֲבוֹתֵינוּ
בַּיָּמִים הָהֵם
בַּזְּמַן הַזֶּה
עַל יְדֵי־כֹּהֲנֶיךָ הַקְּדוֹשִׁים.

וְכָל שְׁמֹנַת יְמֵי חֲנֻכָּה
הַנֵּרוֹת הַלָּלוּ קֹדֶשׁ הֵם
וְאֵין לָנוּ רְשׁוּת לְהִשְׁתַּמֵּשׁ בָּהֶם
אֶלָּא לִרְאוֹתָם בִּלְבָד
כְּדֵי לְהוֹדוֹת
וּלְהַלֵּל לְשִׁמְךָ הַגָּדוֹל
עַל־נִסֶּיךָ
וְעַל־נִפְלְאוֹתֶיךָ
וְעַל־יְשׁוּעָתֶךָ.

ROCK OF ALL MY DREAMS

Maoz Tzur

Rock of all my dreams
I'm anchored in your air
by my heart waking to you
in the house of the world
where these words like answered prayer
are real as conversation:
You built that justice

and the deeper landscape
in which I may walk away
from ruin and despair
and those who would kill me—
rising in all my pasts
to annihilate us—
and into new life

where we imagine a day of completing
a place for you again
in the words we find like new bricks
still warm from the heart's altar—
these words so glad to be at home
they build you a rededication
to match the psalms of Hanukkah.

מָעוֹז צוּר יְשׁוּעָתִי
לְךָ נָאֶה לְשַׁבֵּחַ
תִּכּוֹן בֵּית תְּפִלָּתִי
וְשָׁם תּוֹדָה נְזַבֵּחַ
לְעֵת תָּכִין מַטְבֵּחַ
מִצָּר הַמְנַבֵּחַ
אָז אֶגְמֹר בְּשִׁיר מִזְמוֹר
חֲנֻכַּת הַמִּזְבֵּחַ.

The following short prayer, passage from the Talmud, and psalms are to be spoken while the lights are burning. After Psalm 121, which echoes the recitation of the Hallel in the synagogue, a light-hearted atmosphere reigns until the lights have burned down. During this time, it is traditional for children to receive "Hanukkah money" (or presents) to encourage them to learn more about their Jewish heritage: Hanukkah has traditionally been a time of focus on education. But during this festival no one should be forced to listen or subjected to "education" against his or her will—this is a time for being happy, and children are even allowed to gamble away their Hanukkah money while playing dreidel. This is the only time gambling was sanctioned in Jewish custom, and it is done in the spirit of giddiness at having recovered liberty and the link to a rich past.

WE REMEMBER THE MIRACULOUS

Al Hanissim

We remember the miraculous:
the victories, deliverances, and sudden grace
the inspirations, redemptions, and above all
the wonders of survival and renewal
our mothers and fathers were allowed to see
in ancient days—
they live in our eyes
at these very days of the year

In the days of Mattathias
son of a High Priest, Yohanan—
in the days of this Hasmonean and his sons—
the terrible regime of Greece came
and turned on your people, Israel
to make them forget your words
abandon your ways
and betray the right to be themselves

But you had compassion, you came
to turn their spirit from despair
putting a path before them
a shield beside them
an arm around them

And the strong were delivered
into the hands of the weak
and the many were delivered
into the hands of the few—
iron fists were smashed
by an inner courage
and corruption fell
into hands that were firm—
blind arrogance was delivered
into hands that hold your words
and eyes that read your desire

The deepness of your name arose
shining from the depths of the universe
touching the chord within your people
and in your light Israel found its strength again

miraculously winning its liberty
greeted again with the wonder of being at home
your hand in the world for all to see
and this feeling survives today

Then your children came to the Room of the
      Word
in your House
rededicating the Sanctuary
cleaning the Temple
lighting menorah lights in all the Temple
      courtyards
setting aside these eight days of Hanukkah
for happy psalms and prayers
reflecting the light
touching the chord within
that responds to the depth of your name.

THE TALMUD

Shabbat 21b

What is *Hanukkah?*
According to the Rabbis
Hanukkah begins on the 25th of Kislev
continues for eight days
and no lamentations are to be heard
fasting—for whatever reason—is forbidden

When the Greeks went into the Temple
they desecrated the oil they found there
sanctified for use by the High Priest

When the Maccabeans resisted
and then overcame the Greeks
they found one cruse of sacred oil—
it was overlooked and still lay wrapped
in its sacred seal

When the oil was opened and the Menorah lit
it should have lasted only a day
not enough for a festival
or the time for making a new supply—
and then they found the oil could be relit
for the eight miraculous days

When the following year arrived
these happy days were remembered
becoming a festival of their own
sanctified with the traditional singing
psalms of praise, psalms of thanksgiving.

PSALM FOR MAKING HANUKKAH

Psalm 30

High praises
to you who raised me
up

so my critics fall silent
from their death wishes
over me

Lord Most High
I called you
and I was made new

you pulled me back
from the cold lip of the grave
and I am alive

to sing to you
friends, play in his honor
band of steady hearts

his anger like death
passes in a moment
his love lasts forever

cry yourself to sleep
but when you awake
light is all around you

I thought I was experienced
nothing was going to shake me
I was serious as a mountain

Lord, you were with me and then
you were gone
I looked for your face in terror

my body was made of clay
My Lord, it is now
I call you

what good is my blood my tears
sinking in the mud
is mere dust singing

can it speak
these words on my tongue, Lord
help me

turn my heavy sighing into dance
unbutton my shirt and pants
and wrap me in your glow

so my heart can find its voice
through my lips to you
warm and alive

rising
above all bitterness
high praises.

PSALM FROM A "GREAT HALLEL"

Psalm 121

I look up and find a mountain
to know inside
then light appears

inspired from most high
My Lord, creator
of earth and sky

we shall not be moved
this power inside
never fell asleep

over Israel
My Lord is in the light
the atmosphere

the power that moves my hand
through the sunlight that doesn't melt me
and by the moonlight

that moves us inside
to be inspired
above burning pride

desire
which is the mountain of our life
held in his air

and by his hand
we're free
to be moved

we may come and go
from now
to forever.

from ECCLESIASTES

An Old/New Vision of Hanukkah

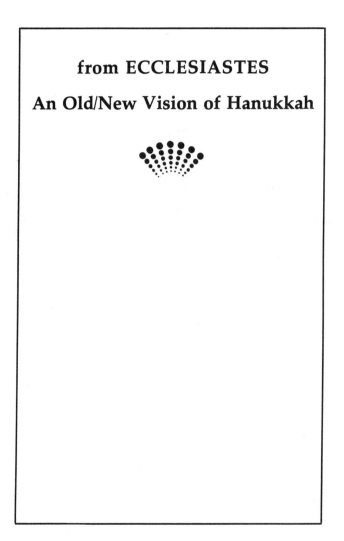

INTRODUCTION

In recent times, passages from Ecclesiastes, like Psalm 121, have been used in Hanukkah programs. In the case of Ecclesiastes, this has more to do with its modern popularity as a piece of "existential" literature than with religious or historical tradition. Still, its biblical authenticity rings truer for the festival than many later sources, first because of its superior literary quality and then because of its spirit of direct confrontation with the world.

But there is another, far more compelling reason for making Ecclesiastes a part of the celebration of Hanukkah. In their efforts to democratize Bible education for the Jewish masses, the "rabbis" of the Maccabean Age divided it into portions for synagogue reading over the year. The books that were known as "scrolls," and considered less fundamental than the Torah or Prophets, were assigned in later times to be read at the biblical festivals. The most popularly known example is the reading of the Book of Esther during Purim. (Ruth is read during Shavuot, Song of Songs during Passover, Lamentations during Tisha b'Av.) Ecclesiastes was assigned to Sukkot, but its association with that festival has been the most tenuous of all, and lately it is all but ignored. Its public reading is

almost unnoticed, if not unknown, in North
America. Since Hanukkah was established in the
spirit of Sukkot, and originally reflected many of its
customs, and since its post-biblical character did not
necessitate a scroll, it seems more than appropriate
to renew the reading of Ecclesiastes—in a modern
context—at Hanukkah. And underlining this connection is the sense of Hanukkah itself as the festival of renewal.

Hanukkah celebrates a cultural renewal that
reanchored the worldwide community of Jews to the
reality of nationhood. And so the modern renewal
of Israel finds a natural analogue in Hanukkah.
Both began with an inspired ethic by a relatively
small group of Jews. The Zionist movement, which
like its Maccabean predecessor may have at first
appeared wildly idealistic, can be seen today, after
the unimaginable murders of the Holocaust, as following a realistic instinct for survival. That instinct
also applies to the Maccabean Age where the indi-
visibility of religious and secular culture was still
the context: what we think of today as religious literature had its secular context as well. As the modern scholar Abraham J. Heschel wrote (in Israel:
An Echo of Eternity [New York, 1969]), "The
Hebrew Bible is not a book about heaven—it is a
book about the earth." And Ecclesiastes, especially
in modern times, has often been thought of as the
most down-to-earth book in the Bible.

The antimaterialistic vision of Ecclesiastes is
often misunderstood because it is rooted in an ap-

preciation of the things of this world. The confusion about its true religious spirit—intensified by its literary sophistication and withering irony—is probably why Ecclesiastes never became popularly associated with the Sukkot festival. Since the religious spirit of Sukkot is one of rejoicing, it takes a subtle understanding to relate this to Ecclesiastes' intense realism. Most of the subtlety about Sukkot has been lost in its adaptation to a secular world. And its spiritual reflection, the festival of Hanukkah, in its very popularity, is vulnerable to oversimplification and trivialization.

The clichés of Hanukkah thrive in North America where the competition with Christmas is greatest. The secular popularity of the Christmas holiday and the commercialization of Christmas spirit make it an attractive model for a Hanukkah severed from its religious value. So it's vital that the original spirit of Hanukkah be emphasized—for instance, in a modern renewal of an ancient literary masterpiece that unites secular and spiritual dimensions.

According to many scholars, Ecclesiastes was composed in the third century B.C.E., preceding the Maccabean era by less than a hundred years. More likely, it dates from the seventh century B.C.E. In either case, most of its material, which is virtually quoted by the poet, is even older, and perhaps dates back to King Solomon (tenth century B.C.E.). Solomon is the author of Ecclesiastes according to tradition, and it's fitting he be represented in the Hanukkah literature, as David is by Psalm 30.

As with most biblical texts, there are in a sense two layers (not without additional sublayers) to the composition: the older one contains oral or written sources in fragmentary form, and the later one represents the vision of the composer (centuries later) who set down the text close to the way we now have it. That is an oversimplification, but it helps describe my own method of working. I tried to recreate the depth inherent in a text spanning centuries by juxtaposing traditional and contemporary imagery. If I emphasize the psychological perspective, it's because it is the one most easily lost in translation; the same can be said for the pervasive sense of irony, when homilies and clichés that are being intentionally defrocked come out sounding in translation like the cliché itself.

In an important sense, the book is not just telling us about life, but actually demonstrating its approach in a poetry blending skepticism with faith. In this sense it is both a Jewish critique of the pagan genre known as "wisdom literature," and a more subtle commentary on specifically Jewish conventions of wisdom literature. More simply, Ecclesiastes is scathing in its attitude to any form of idolatry, pagan or literary. Yet in confronting the relentless vanities of life and literature head on, the poet never loses a sense of joy in both. This joy is grounded in the same faith that attaches Ecclesiastes to Sukkot and Hanukkah.

In some medieval Jewish ghettoes, there was a time when Hanukkah celebrations resembled the

Purim masquerades. The atmosphere of giddy parody corresponded to the sense of relief at having survived grim threats of destruction, whether the emphasis was on physical annihilation as at Purim, or cultural and spiritual annihilation as at Hanukkah. Preserving the giddy sense of having survived is another, though not a major, dimension that compliments the realism of Ecclesiastes. Yet Hanukkah commemorates not just the survival of Jewish people but the ability of Judaism to transform itself. The further proof that its inner core of strength was immovable enhanced a faith in inevitable renewal throughout history. And if there's an abiding theme of Ecclesiastes, it is the inevitability of renewal.

This renewal does not descend from heaven, but cannot come solely from personal initiative either. Kohelet's (the pseudononymous author of Ecclesiastes—also its Hebrew title) attack on wisdom and experience itself corresponds to the Jewish resistance of the prevailing Greek wisdom in Maccabean times. He transforms the popular "success-oriented" wisdom of his day, as well as the dogmatic clichés of religious wisdom, by anchoring them in naked awareness. His composition is poetic in its ceaseless ebbing and flowing, its renewals, rather than arriving at a logical program—it depicts the process of awareness. It embraces the world while attacking materialistic values and is an emblem of Hanukkah spirit for our success-oriented culture today.

from ECCLESIASTES

Then I looked up
above my personal horizon
to see the sky

outstretching the sea
as wisdom
lightens a heavy body

a wise man's eyes
are in his head
while the absent-minded

professor or egoist
disdains to wipe his glasses
while he sinks to the bottom of the sea

but wisdom as quickly evaporates
the moment a body dies
shipwrecked beneath its headstone

the most penetrating realist
hits rock bottom
six feet under

and the farthest seer
on the beachhead of life
gets his mouthful of sand

152

so even wisdom is a pocket
turned inside out
when it's time to pay the body's burden

the blind will lead the wise
beyond the furthest suburb of memory
into total obscurity

reentering the city of the future
as dust to be swept away
from the pages of the present

so where will I go
with this wisdom   this breath
in the sail of a fool

and so I turned again
blind as a hurricane
against the sea of life

where all works sink
like jettisoned cargo
under the lidless eyeball of the sun

the whole cargo of civilization
was a weight on my shoulders
my life's work dead weight

all life depressingly empty
hollow as cardboard dumbbells
in a bad circus

a bad dream
in which my fame honor wealth
all the earnings disappeared in a thought

in a dream circus where a clown waited
cocky in his painted face
of identity

to inherit all my works
and I am not to know
if there's a mind and heart of depth

beneath the greasepaint
or it really is the face
of life's unrelenting sideshow

in which my successor my reader
discounts my lifework
in a snobbish indifference

to the working man   common or
artist (and helmsman
of the direction life has dealt him

in working his will over it)
and my books my record
fade and crack in the sun

cast overboard like ballast
all that I've learned not even a shadow
cast in the desert

a little shade for integrity
my wealth empty as a mirage
of water

and so my heart sank
to the bottom
in the dry well of despair

empty of illusions
about the fine sweat we produce
under the sun

slave to a desire
for *whose* "one fine day"?
each day another sigh

accumulated
another groan for the harvest
of rich disappointment

each night
our hearts lie wide awake
lashed to the body's ship

ferrying that load of heartache
from day to day
with the constant of breathing

to fill the sail
and ripple the pages
of an empty book

the best thing for a man
is to eat drink and be
just be

satisfaction in the flow
of works and days
as it is all the work

of a creator
making me
aware of my body

and by its satisfaction
my need to be here
a pen in the hand of the Lord—

who will feel the pressure
of his will
if not I?

and if what I do is pleasing
in his eyes
I will see through my own

a work graced with beauty
a world open
to a fresh page of understanding

on which I create
my own happiness
an articulate self-knowledge

and if I project
only my own vision
with my tiny primitive hand-driven will

I will be the ancestral hunter
and gatherer   a slave
to the stalking of wealth and power

and the snobbish mask of nobility
the illusion of living
(in ignorance) forever

which at my death will be handed over
to another man   an open one
deep enough to hold his fortune within

fulfilling his creator
in the reality of commerce
between vision and self-awareness

adding a living dimension
to the flat mirror
of the future

the mirror in which puffed-up
self-centered lords
are drowning in vanity.

(2:13–26)

There is time for everything to happen
under the sun   to lift anchor
in the flow of seasons

everything has its moment
under the uncounted stars
its season of desire

summer of being born
winter of dying
spring of seeding

fall of reaping
winter of killing
summer of healing

spring of uprooting
fall of rebuilding
fall of weeping

spring of laughing
winter of lamenting
summer of dancing

summer making love
winter of surviving
spring of embracing

fall of parting
spring of finding
fall of losing

winter keeping
summer discarding
summer of hot tears

winter of consoling
winter of silence
summer speaking out

spring in love
fall in anger
winter of war

and hating
summer of peace
and hugging

but what can a man add
to the interworking of things
of his own intrinsic value

is a man anything different
whether or not the sweat and thought
is wrung from his body like a rag

I have thought about the tatters
and felt the finest mindspun silk
these are clothes created for us

all men and women wear them
the work of their creator
who has dressed everything in space

each event in time
tailored to its place
and he puts a mannequin of desire

before the hearts and minds of men
so that we long to dress ourselves
create a vision of the future

in which our lives fit today
with a similar beauty of rightness
but the longing for a world of our own

defeats us   the world defeats us
like a mirror we may not look behind
though a taste of creation propels us forward

I have seen as with a long look
the best a man can make
is to create his own goodness

out of a clear image of himself
the satisfaction in simply being alive
the pleasure of his own eyes

seeing
as long as he can
as long as he lives

just to eat and drink
the fruits of your work
is a gift from your creator

the world is a gift that lasts
he gave
and nothing more can be added

no matter can be erased
the universe beyond us
came before us

and the wonder of our presence
is that we feel it all
in the awe before our own little creations

in the awe of our hearts moving
closer to their creator
as we ourselves become stiller

the grace to be still
in the flow of all creation
for a moment

and through the window of a moment
the opening of eyes within eyes
to see the ancient perspective of time

painted in a landscape with light
the future the eyelids opening
as of a prehistoric creature

under the ungraspable sky
that was
is

and will be: the airless height
of understanding   pure space we pursue
like fish the worms of conscience

and are drawn to
like a seed to air
in a new baby's wail

like a man to a woman
like a creature
to his maker

(3:1–15)

Watch your step
when your feet automatically carry you
unconsciously   to the temple

it's better to see yourself
and feel
what you are doing

than offer blind obedience
but go in
with your eyes open

and keep your heart open
to the right way
don't lead your heart blindly

into a marriage of convenience
don't be a fool   except for love
of the truth

and then you will know
what you love
and if you must suffer it

the pain will have some value
you'll know how to carry that weight
inside   your arms still open

to hold the life
you are given
as your own

those who watch their hearts
before they take a step
walk into sleeves of darkness

their hearts comfortably dressed
for the time they sacrifice to religion
walking down that narrow aisle

so richly upholstered   a tunnel
sealed against the life flowing
from the real temple's spirit

it is too dimly lit there
for them to know
what good or evil they are married to.

(4:17–18)

But don't open your mouth
too quickly or spill out your heart
in an alphabet soup of prayers

his vision spreads across heaven
where a mouthful of words aren't needed
and you are on earth

where words can come cheaply
to someone so low to the ground
he can't foresee the next minute

the next second when suddenly
his mood changes
and he is denying what he just said

bad dreams daydreams fantasies
spread like blinding steam
from too much living in the moment

too many things to do
with no pause for real reflection
and hot air streams from the mouth

of someone who talks too much
if you've promised to do something
if you've sworn to God

do it
he has less time than you have
to sit in the steambath

and wish the world away
pay what you owe even as it pains
and your eyes will clear a path for you

better yet don't make promises
you can't keep
especially to yourself: it's your mouth

in your body
so don't let it betray
flesh of your flesh

and when you do
and when the messenger comes to collect on it
take your foot out of your mouth

don't pretend it was perfectly natural
to mistakenly be licking someone's foot
don't pretend your mouth is not in your head

but respect the work of your creator
who put it there   he is perfectly right
to be angry with your swollen voice

and to puncture the blister of things
you've accumulated around you
with the grasping hands

he also presented to you
along with the gift of language
you infect with mouths of stale air

from the disembodied chatter
of fantasies and dreams
false gods and persons

streaming from the unchecked mind
inflating the world with unreal messages—
wake up   and trust your maker.

(5:1–6)

A lover led by silver
will never embrace enough of her
his arms won't even reach behind her

and one in love with more
than he can hold
gets only more of the same: frustration

and another vain kiss the wind
blows away
like seed not firmly planted

in a body of earth
a measure equal
to a body's need

the more food the land produces
the more people grow up
to eat it

what satisfaction is this easy multiplication
to the stomach of its owner
who grows fat in the eyes

feasting on his own desire
to be bright and superior
in the social mirror

of shallow eyes
a surface flattened for respect
adding up to a fat reflection

while the undistracted worker
tired from sheer indivisible labor
melts into sleep

like a cube of sugar
in a glass of tea
regardless of what he's eaten

but the man bloated with possessions
living in a dream-stomach of selfhood
a pig of identity

this man digesting property
indiscriminately as a camel
in the garbage dumps on the outskirts

of Beersheba
this rich man with a full stomach
inside and outside

gulping the wine of self-imagery
and still this man just can't fall asleep
his peace sits at the bottom of his glass

a lump of stone
and the man who hides his wealth
like the man who lives alone

grows sick on the stale breath of himself
ends up in a daydream
where he tosses away his fortune

in an impulsive fit
and the hoard of his ego
falls to pieces within him

nothing to pass on
to his son   the milk soured in the heat
of a sudden passionate thought

his hand empty
the glass shattered on the floor
rock bottom   the pit

naked and wet
as when he came through
the womb where he was fashioned

and he will follow his mother
back again to a deeper
source in earth

the mother of us all
stripped to the dry skeleton
barest image of a human

falling back
into the hidden hand
of creation

his own hands slowly unforming
and all that they held
all the land and fruits

of labor   gone
another daydream gone sour
another life led down the path

into a falling darkness
another illusion for the instincts
naked he came naked returns

alone with his reality
a life struggling to grasp
something in the wind

to make something more
of his own breath
than the spirit his efforts obscure

the labor that eats away inside
like another hungry worker
toiling away in the darkness inside

this companion worker this utter
reality   born in frustration
in a fertile mind   bred in worry and anger

and this is what I learned
what's worth struggling to learn
is as beautiful as being

working to eat drink and be
satisfied in the flow
of works and days

like water shining under the sun
harnessed
to the energy burning within

the little sun of a lifetime
God has given   so
let's have a good time

in the simple space and time
of human vision
that I may hold

in my hands
like a telescope
the fact of memory

embracing the world
with the feeling of real arms
warm from their labor

and to those of us allowed
luxury and property and
grace to enjoy them

in this gift of a body
happy in the sun
on a smooth shore of a life

content by the glistening sea
of our own fine sweat
which brought us to a home we feel good in—

that home is a vessel
a gift of God
in which we travel awhile

a little journey equal to the breadth
of our vision
the depth of our memory

a present to us
buoyant on the waves
connecting past and future

the surges of wind and breath
keeping a mind clear
through dark passages of fear

that life is passing us by
blood washing over stone
making us rigid with fear   stone

but God makes a clearing in the heart
we gather our thoughts there   a labor
mirroring the work that reveals us to ourselves.

(5:10–5:20)

Anything that has a beginning
everything
was a seed in the pot

planted before existence
and named by men
as it flowed into the world

man is also a kind of flower
whose growth is defined
and all that flows from his hands

and with our own little names
we can't argue with our creator
a name that's boundless

beyond identity
like death which takes back our names
and gives them to the living

the more words we use
the more bricks for the mausoleum
building castles in the air

that are ancient relics
the moment we exhale
passed on to ignorant children

when we die
they prefer sand castles
and when the tide comes in they will not cry

but watch   fascinated
no better or worse
than all preceding men

who knows
what the right thing to do is
with a life

that walks across a stage
of air
in a bathing costume of flesh

until night falls like a gown
over a beautiful woman
who sleeps alone

only our shadows remain
impotent watchmen
on the shore of the life

our blood flowed to
and suddenly they too are gone
as the sun again rises

piercing all wishes and dreams
and romances of the future
with the bones of light

we are stripped awake   leaving
a shadow on the shore
that had not seen its own body.

(6:10–12)

A Note on Translation and Liturgy

A NOTE ON TRANSLATION AND LITURGY

Creative translations are necessary to open the Jewish heritage to those who feel it is a closed book. Whether they can or cannot read Hebrew, many people feel alienated from the essence of Jewish practice and imagination.

There is a long Jewish tradition of creative translations from Hebrew into the contemporary idiom, in numerous languages from ancient Aramaic (where they are known as "Targums") to modern Yiddish. Yiddish was the immigrant language of most American Jews and though its usage has died away there have been few attempts to make popular translations of the Jewish heritage into an English that is not an englishified "Biblespeak."

Why have American poets and novelists been so rarely called upon to translate Jewish literature, when it was not uncommon for American Yiddish writers to creatively interpret traditional works barely fifty years ago? Why does prayerbook after prayerbook contain translations which are indifferent to the American tongue? Meanwhile, academic translators distinguish themselves in modern approaches to the Hebrew, but are intimidated by the imaginative resources of English.

Whenever the majority of Jews in any given time and place had grown alienated from the Hebrew language, creative translations and interpretations were abundant—their very creativity insured that they would not be mistaken for the great Hebrew original. They also helped to discredit the wild teachings of fanatics and literalists. Now that English is the only language in which the majority of American Jews are fluent, it seems natural to link up with the Jewish heritage by approaching it in a creative idiom—and always with the intention of reinforcing the authenticity of the original Hebrew. So I've worked toward a text that can be spoken aloud with a resonance in English that mirrors biblical poetry. By using the lines and stanzas of modern poetry—which has been a lifework—I try to suggest the rhythm and phrasing of a spoken idiom.

Reflecting the Hebrew, I've used a minimum of punctuation. I've felt in many cases that an expansiveness of imagery is necessary to do justice to the inspired intensity of the Hebrew. A modern word-for-word translation produces a grossly inaccurate picture of the original poetic texture, especially in the quality of Hebrew metaphor. Perhaps not since the sixteenth-century idiom of Elizabethan England has an inventive richness been allowed that does not devalue the Hebrew.

Resisting the easy allure of sacred idols, the Jewish imagination breathes deeply in the imagery of language. Scholars can translate a sense of the Hebrew in various shades of clarity, but they are not trained to evoke the immediacy of feeling in the original. By reaching for a measure of literary integrity in English, I've allowed myself the freedom to use sometimes more— and occasionally fewer—words than the usual translations. But I've never omitted a Hebrew word—the spacing device in some lines of Zechariah and Ecclesiastes is used to pace the reader and dramatize the spoken rhythm. I've wanted to be true to the original atmosphere of the texts and not to a concept of diction that would embarrass a wooden Indian.

When it comes to certain key words, I've translated them with an ear for modern relevance. For instance, the root term "mitzvah" was translated as "commandment" a hundred years ago and no real alternative for the subtle variations in its usage has been offered to this day, even though the modern resonance of "commandment" is quite different from the earlier, spiritual one. In certain places, I've translated it as "desire," which is more accurate in its contemporary context, as well as an illumination (I hope) of the original Hebrew. It is the attention to accuracy of the heart and ear that makes a contemporary renewal of liturgical translation possible.